CERTAINTY LOST: A
hollow romance

CERTAINTY LOST: A hollow romance

Alone in a dark, cold, lonely universe

Jack Dikian

To Bud, my old beagle who taught me how to think straight about being human.

"We are like butterflies that flutter for a day and think it is forever."

– Carl Sagan

Author's note

I have come to a serious realization that objectivity is a myth, at best a rarity. I think it was a romantic idea from the very beginning, that a person can look at a fact and see it for what it is. Facts are facts. They can be numbers, they can be things, objects, even UFOs. They should be easy enough to appreciate and accept as they are. In fact, they may be to the human mind, but hardly to the human person.

For a long time, I must have become somewhat lazy, preferring to take the path of least resistance, especially with what we call facts, knowledge, and truth. It had become easy to believe that what I see, hear and learn are facts, knowledge and truth – and anything to the contrary is false. After all, I have had extensive experience, having lived all of four decades and, perhaps, an extraordinary exposure to people, events and places that the majority of people don't have. I always had good grades in subjects I wanted to study, and a quick, instinctive or intuitive grasp of what's what in life. Also, I had reasonable courage to face hard truths, especially my shortcomings.

Because I write, and more importantly, I read, I am always engaged with the unlimited spectrum of human imagination and artistry. Many writers can have such unimaginable creativity, snatching thought images from nowhere and everywhere, that they are making life so enthralling and thrilling to those who read them. Many more have such gift with words that I am stunned by how they manipulate language from just being informative to being simply awesome. My heroes include the Bard, F. Scott Fitzgerald, and Ernest Hemingway to name a few. These writers who have such intelligence and profound insights, these writers who use words like music and dance, they make up for everything else.

Today credulity among the public for tales of the astonishing is less than even a generation ago. The standard explanation attributes this to a growing scepticism. But scepticism alone is a convenient short-hand for a deeper psycho-social, historical and cultural phenomenon spanning the duration of the last two centuries. The UFO spectacle sits alongside the manifestation of a visual consumer culture; acquiring the dimensions of an alternative reality and reflecting the breakdown of the distinction between what was once the visible and the invisible, the material and the spiritual, the phenomenal and the noumenal.

This hallow culture replaced the dull, grey world with its own, phantasmatic iridescence. It mattered nought whether or not everybody genuinely could buy a part of the universal plenty. What mattered was the mythology, the illusion of bountiful possibility and limitless choice, wrapped up in a spectacularity borrowed from the film and television industries.

When the social theorists of the Frankfurt School arrived in New York during their wartime exile in the 1930s, they found the giant billboard ads for toothpaste even more-nerve jangling than they had expected. Here was a culture entirely mortgaged to the secular spectacular. In previous centuries, what was visually remarkable stood for the other-worldly, the spiritual.

The baroque façades and soaring spires of cathedrals, the carmines and cobalts of stained-glass windows with the sun streaming through them, devotional processions and carnival parades, gargoyles, misericords, miraculous relics — all attested that there was an intangible reality beyond the physical one, a reality that could at most be suggestively delineated in extraordinary sights.

The impulse against the visual culture, however, was buoyed by the very fact that they can be seen, and importantly, bore traces of human artifice. But, where people were convinced that they had seen the other world impinging on material reality, or were persuaded that others had, the connection between what one could see and what one might believe grew deeper.

Materialisations of the Blessed Virgin at Lourdes in France, at Knock in Ireland, and at Fátima in Portugal, suggested that the visions of the first Christians — those who not only saw but spoke to, ate with and touched their risen Lord — were still available for anyone with eyes to see.

What these countervailing powers have brought about in postmodern society is a different kind of scepticism. A large element of rationalist doubt, certainly, accompanies the decline of interest in the paranormal, driven primarily by these cultural and, latterly, technological factors. Yet underlying that doubt itself is the growing incredulity with which people evaluate anything and everything.

Supermarket discounts appear to offer wines at half-price; products for smearing on your face purport to make you look younger — these are the all-too-evident mendacities. The homilies of party politicians at election time sound like the exclamatory drivel of public relation companies. And the way this stuff has permeated culture as a whole has bred a widespread incurious scepticism. We now extend the same degree of undifferentiating refusal even to those phenomena that, while hard to credit, deserve to be heeded.

Contemporary scepticism takes the role of playing along with the clamour because there seems to be no alternative, while privately knowing that it can't deliver what it promises. In this cast of mind, somebody's hyperventilating tale of a translucent glow seen drifting high in the night sky, or the disembodied footsteps that clatter up and down the stairs when everybody is tucked up in bed, is neither more nor less believable than the weather forecast. The dignity of spooky stories was that, unlike obvious tissues of lies, they occasionally managed to cross the divide between the highly unlikely and the just barely credible. If they could never be proved, neither could they ever be disproved.

The visible and the invisible, the material and the spiritual, the phenomenal and the noumenal are no longer the distinct realms they once were. They have become mutually permeable to their mutual diminishment. We seem to see to the heart of things, to what Kant knew as the thing-in-itself, to a degree undreamed of at the high-water mark of pure reason in the 18th century.

The cameras of natural history programming miss nothing, even at the cellular level, even in pitch dark, and yet everything looks like the video that it is. There are those who continue to believe the Moon landings were a hoax just because the film evidence looks so fake and could so easily have been produced in a studio.

By contrast, the notorious black-and-white extraterrestrial autopsy footage from Roswell, New Mexico is an insultingly obvious fraud, as educated people reassured each other at the film's emergence in 1995, having forgotten for a moment that the absurdity lay not in the cinematography but in the very idea of an extraterrestrial.

This is a book about professed extraterrestrials, the visually remarkable, seen, accessible - sentient beings received from out of space, from other worlds.

But this is a book mostly about us, people like you and I. How we have come to forge belief and what countervailing powers bring about certainty and doubt. In the classic mise-en-scène, at remote, deserted locations, country roads or woodland at nights: UFO sightings reflect our yearning of what may lay beyond, romanticised impresses of more civilised lives, of wonder, imagination, anticipation and the unknown - all at once in opposition with incredulity, suspicion and doubt.

Contents

"If the stars should appear one night in a thousand years, how would men believe and adore; and preserve for many generations the remembrance of the city of God which had been shown! But every night come out these envoys of beauty, and light the universe with their admonishing smile."

Ralph Waldo Emerson,
Nature and Selected Essays

1.   How small we are

Gazing out into the vastness of a starry sky is a sobering confrontation, one we've strived to understand since the dawn of man. That black, maddening firmament; that vast cosmic ocean, endlessly deep in every direction, both heaven, and pandemonium at once.

The North star, unremitting, one of man's most steady guides, looking upon us in our days of haste and waiting for us there when we have gotten old when we have lived all that we can live, a lifetime of joys and a lifetime of hopes. When Shakespeare looked up at the stars, he said of fair Juliet, "brightness of her cheek would shame those stars." Everything we know, love, hate, see, think of, obsess over or imagine lies on this tiny world floating imperceptibly in the outliers of space.

Imagine our Sun as a single grain of sand. Our Sun is one of a multitude of stars. It's surrounded by over 200 billion stars in our own Milky Way galaxy alone. Our sun is just a speck in the vast beach of stars. But the Milky Way galaxy is itself just one of 100 billion galaxies scattered across the Cosmos. It has been estimated that there are more stars in the universe than there are grains of sand in all the beaches in all the world.

Man gazed upwards from this rocky and unremarkable post, a place of life, and began to make reckoning, slowly at first, of virtue and godly life, and reading of omens in the sky, a mean to secure the state. Some relied on well-established calendars to anticipate floods; rituals were required to be able to tell the time during the night. Aristotle reasoned the Earth was round, he wrote:

> *"Indeed, there are some stars seen in Egypt and in the neighbourhood of Cyprus which are not seen in the northerly regions; and stars, which in the north are never beyond the range of observation, in those regions rise and set. All of which goes to show not only that the earth is circular in shape, but also that it is a sphere of no great size: for otherwise the effect of so slight a change of place would not be quickly apparent."*

> Aristotle: Book 2, Chapter 14, 340 BC

How we came to understand reality at the largest scale is, in my mind, one of humanities' greatest accomplishment. In the last one-hundred years, mankind has performed a miracle, truly explaining the origins of man, the origins of the universe, how did we come to be here and where might we be going.

But Man achieved much looking inward too. The acceptance of human rights, the recognition of the inherent dignity and of the equal and inalienable rights of all members of the human race - the foundation of freedom, justice and peace in the world. The invention of the Gutenberg press, the catalyst of the renaissance, scientific revolution, enlightenment, and the Modern Age.

The theory of evolution, completely altered our understanding of how organisms relate, change and came to be. It asks one of the most provocative questions... what are we? From what did we come? What will we become? The domestication of fire helped us cook, carried additional glucose to the brain, increased the size of our brain. The creation of vaccines and widespread vaccination programmes have led to the decline and extinction of dangerous diseases, polio, Tuberculosis, smallpox and others.

In the beginning was the Big Bang. We know now that the universe arose from a single point, a point prior to which was nothing; during which and after, something: the universe and everything. The universe sprang into existence from nothingness and into somethingness. We're able to calculate back to an instant when it was smaller than the diameter of an electron, we can't go back further than that. That last picosecond, a pre-physical epoch, a singularity in space and time, science cannot explain. That spark didn't appear in space; rather it created space. Indeed, the Big Bang was a moment in time, not a point in space. It didn't expand into the void; it was the void. Here the grammatical structure of our language works against us, since it assumes, we are talking about something happening in space-time.

But why – why a Big Bang - indeed, why a universe at all, and why stop at just one, perhaps inevitable, perhaps it is precisely what is needed of the universe - a universe compelled to eventually have us emerge within. A strong anthropic principle, we can't explicate. All we really know is that we are inside it and at one point it wasn't there and then in a flash it materialised, literally, from nothing and from nowhere. Was God the "Prime directive," this book can't say. Many have asked the question and many more so believe he made it so. There could be much outside our expanding universe, our observable universe, quite possibly even other universes, but that's not for us to behold - we can't. What we see today is all that we are ever going to see.

If we scale the whole history of the universe to a single year, humans wouldn't appear till December 31, 11.59pm on New Year's Eve. On the same timescale we have observed the universe for only a fraction of a second, yet we made much bold conclusions – not always possible.

How little we are, inside. Every one of us on Earth, every Nation and Region, all living beings. We are a part of one, a large, but insignificantly small. And while some believe we are at the centre of all, the most important thing - the truth is that we can't grasp it all. We may never will. The distances in space are unimaginably vast - beyond our comprehension, beyond reach. The Universe is not just stranger than we imagine — it is stranger than we can imagine.

Millions of years later, after the Big Bang, stars started to contract under their own weight, their cores, now in the order of several millions of degrees, began burning Hydrogen, the most abundant and lightest fuel; fusing it into Helium and producing light – star light. All the atoms that exist today, hydrogen, oxygen, calcium, all the atoms that go into forming the chemicals necessary for life were cooked in the crucibles of space and forged in the cauldrons of stars. Romantically, we can say, we are all made of stars, star-dust.

Given this, given the vastness of space, the countless number of stars, opportunities for life; a most important question can be asked – is it plausible that we could be alone? Or, are there others like us, other sentient beings, other civilizations, other hopes and dreams, other life. I think not.

2. A little town called Rachel

Not more than about 100 miles North of Las Vegas in the Great Basin Desert, along Nevada Highway 375, nicknamed the world's loneliest highway lies a small town of Rachel. Surrounded by flat, open scrubland and bordered by distant hilltops, the town; a gas station, a bar, a few rickety trailers parked just off the main road.

One can drive for miles and see not a living thing. The relentless flatness of the landscape is broken only by the sporadic scattering of undergrowth and menacing triffid-like Joshua trees rising out of the earth. The only traffic is the occasional truck – tranquillity disturbed, on the dreary desert road, distant trucks hang in the haze, an amalgam of dust against a blistering sun. During the day, visibility is great, but at dusk and at night, locals warn, rabbits are most active, and cows will wander on to the road.

The town wasn't always called Rachel. And, for it not to have been a stone's throw from the nearby Nellis Air Force Base, the tiny town with a population of around 100 would be just another town – a desolate high desert town. Activity revolving mostly around ranching, mining, and farming. In Rachel, in the fading afternoon light, buzzards drift lazily, bullet holes let the sun stream through and around decrepit, twisted signposts - a clue to idleness, a life in a small town. There are some tracks of life - a couple of teenagers circle an iron drum on bikes, a scrawny dog tired and fast asleep. Tired of searching deserts for companions from before, his master doesn't whistle tunes, he isn't in the mood, the unabating air is too still.

Rachel a conservative, mostly Baptist, stand by their provincial view. A community of folk related or met at early at school. They hold to likewise ideals, sentiments, stake little in those just passing through. But Rachel isn't just another small town. After it was founded in May 1973 by a local alfalfa farmer, the town was renamed from Sand Springs to Rachel after the birth of the first baby in the high valley, Rachel Jones. Rachel, the girl didn't live long enough to see her town become a household name, she died at the age of three on May 23, 1980.

A facility about 25 miles South of Rachel can be approached from two directions. One approach, close to Rachel, takes the visitor down approximately 6 miles of a winding dirt roads, to a guard building and gate in the middle of nowhere. The other approach is 14 miles down Groom Lake Road, at the base of Hancock Summit. The turnoff, marked only by a lone stop sign, is here: 37.414741°, -115.409875°. Signs at the gate and border point warn travellers that any attempt to enter the base will be met with fines, prison time, or even deadly force. This is the United States Air Force facility commonly known as Area 51, a highly classified remote detachment of Edwards Air Force Base, within the Nevada Test and Training Range.

We don't exactly know what goes on at this facility. We probably never will. Paradoxically, this isn't necessarily an altogether bad thing. Sometimes, facts can dull the imagination. Moreover, conspiracy beliefs are part of an evolved psychology; a mechanism specifically aimed at detecting coalitions, perilous confederacies – an argued source of value, an attribute of survival.

This assumes that conspiracy theories are activated after specific coalition cues, which produce functional counterstrategies to cope with suspected conspiracies. Insights from social, cultural and evolutionary psychology provide tentative support for this proposition and follow from the adaptation hypothesis.

People possess a functionally integrated mental system to detect conspiracies that in all likelihood has been shaped in an ancestral human environment in which hostile coalitions - that is, conspiracies that truly existed were a frequent cause of misery, death, and reproductive loss.

And, we're not programmed for truth – we are programmed for survival. There are smells around that we physically can't smell, there are sights to witness beyond the wavelength that our eyes operate in, and there are sounds to be heard that we will never fully hear. The reason for this is that these things aren't required for us to pass on our genes.

The environments that we adapted to didn't need us to be able to see like a snake might be able to or to sniff to the extent that a dog can.

Given the historical evidence and given all that's been divulged it's highly indicatory that the installation, an employ of the US government, serves as an active testing ground for the most clandestine, cutting-edge, if not conventional and most secretive of the experimental aircraft, stealth technology, advanced weapons, electronic warfare systems and, in particular, unmanned aerial vehicles.

Secrecy is nothing new. Governments excel at eluding the prying questions of the people. Who can blame them? Secrets have always created a kind of motivational conflict. Avoiding the social costs accompanying unpopular pronouncements conflict with maintaining trustworthy connections. Governmental secrets are no exception. Secrets are powerful, and so are open deportments - but all too often, secrecy seems like the path of the least resistance.

Our ability to justify everything we have to say is exactly how we become trapped into the "we" we aren't actually able to be. Of course, where there are secrets, conspiracies, cover-ups and repression, there are rumours and there is gossip. We love telling stories, we like to gossip. We can't help it - gossip has been an integral to our survival. Our language evolved specifically so as to enable us to gossip. Since the time of early man, our ancestors have used gossip as a social means to keep one another in line and to get along.

Secrets can also keep us safe – they are the sturdy walls we erect within and around ourselves, keeping us trapped, wrapped, in a narrow sliver of certainty in which we find content. This is never more than the case than during a crisis. In an era of cold-war relations, Dwight Eisenhower sought to pursue a heightened national commitment to counter the spread of Soviet insurgency. Eschewing the costly, conventional ground forces of the Truman presidency, and wielding the vast superiority of the U.S. nuclear arsenal and covert intelligence - "brinksmanship."

Government disclosure of its own video footage, for example, isn't helping to maintain belief. It's actually better for UFOs when ufologists can claim that the powers that be know everything and are hiding it from us rather than seeing that the government appears to have basically the same info about UFOs as the public: namely grainy, inconclusive visual evidence. But even here, conspiracy theory finds a way to sneak through. Chapter Nine discusses the decline of UFO sightings – one reason given is the possibility that reports to UFO organisations are being intercepted electronically by government organisations.

At this time, the CIA and Lockheed needed a place to test their top-secret spy plane, the U-2. It is instructive to note that Lockheed skunk works founder Kelly Johnson was not one to squander an opportunity. He tells his people, "Now, listen. I want to take the company Bonanza and find us a place our on the desert somewhere where we can test this thing in secret..." there was no extraterrestrial enchantment, just good-old American capitalism and necessary technological protectionism.

I should mention of another argument - that is, that of state sovereignty as we understand it is anthropocentric, or "constituted and organized by reference to human beings alone." The real reason UFOs have been dismissed is because of the existential challenge that they pose for a worldview in which human beings are the most technologically advanced life-forms.

Rachel - the intense secrecy surrounding the base has, predictably, made it the frequent subject of many conspiracy theories and a central component to unidentified flying object folklore. Since trying to get into Area 51 will land you in prison, the nearby one-bar town of Rachel has, with little rivalry, become to be an unlikely basecamp of sorts. As far as base camps go, Rachel has its own social structure.

The bar, the Little A 'Le' Inn, a restaurant and gift shop, stocks the obligatory curious and curiouser's essentials: beer, coffee, coffee mugs, bumper stickers, bug-eyed alien dolls, and t-shirts. Locals on hand regale tales of mysterious sonic booms and skies washed with persistent blooms. It's hard to find anyone who doesn't claim to have had some kind of paranormal experience. Even the beliefs of the self-confessed sceptics are more ambiguous and irrational than would normally be heard on the Clapham omnibus.

But first, they will all turn around. They will want to take a look at who enters their inn, eventually, quietly returning to their thoughts and returning to their woes. Not far from Rachel, just to the west, there's another attraction. The Alien Cathouse, advertised as the only alien-themed brothel in Armagosa, Nevada. Apparently, the ladies are amazing, and patrons are encouraged to let their fantasies run wild because the sky has no limitation.

Some 30 years ago, an engineer named Bob Lazar claimed to have climbed onboard an alien spaceship. He watched flying saucers dart over Papoose Lake and the Tikaboo Valley. Lazar told a Las Vegas television reporter George Knapp that he saw autopsy photographs of aliens (called "kids") inside the facility and that the U.S. government used the facility to examine recovered extraterrestrial spacecraft. His story, an exclusive, aired on Las Vegas television in 1989 and soon become an overnight sensation.

Years later, Lazar, tells of his work with the United States army. As it turns out something quite mundane as far as engineering work is concerned. Why build bridges, locks and dams, when you can get to tinker with an extraterrestrial spaceship. The official task; to reverse engineer the power and propulsion system, oh, and to figure out if we can build one like it.

In the *2018 feature-length documentary Bob Lazar: Area 51 & Flying Saucers*, Lazar gave an expansive interview. Amongst other things, he explains the inner workings of the Earth-fairing extraterrestrial spaceship. Look, I'm just going to throw this out there with, hopefully little provocation – make of it what you will. For fun, one of the two extracts below is taken from popular science fiction. The other, from an engineer, no less from the United States army.

> ".... warp engines were fuelled by the reaction of matter (deuterium) and antimatter (anti-deuterium), mediated through an assembly of Dilithium crystals, which were nonreactive with antimatter when subjected to high-frequency electromagnetic fields. This reaction produced a highly energetic plasma, called electro-plasma or warp plasma, which was channelled by plasma conduits through the electro-plasma system (EPS); that system also provided the primary energy supply for the ships other electronic systems. For propulsion the electro-plasma was funnelled by plasma injectors into a series of warp field coils, usually

located in remote warp nacelles. These coils were composed of Verterium cortenide generated the warp field..."

––––––

"... the 'sports model'; directly above each one is a small rectangular object. This is on the floor above, and these are the gravity amplifiers themselves. Looking down from the top you'd have the centre. And in the centre, there is a small reactor. Surrounding this, in three equally spaced areas are the amplifiers. Under the amplifiers, underneath the floor below are the gravity emitters. So, it's the reactor here, powering the gravity amplifiers. Gravity amplifiers' output goes into the gravity emitters at the bottom, and the resulting gravity beam or anti-gravity wave can be pretty much put anywhere you want to.

Um., there was there version of a computer or something to make determinations here that takes inputs from those sensors and then let the craft know how to orient itself and where it was in space. The centre antenna is really an extension of the reactor (antimatter) in the centre. And that's a wave guide which allows the emission of the gravity wave which forms kind of a heart shape over the whole craft. That's how it creates its distortion. These gravity emitters can be swung all the way up to 180 degrees and this allows the craft to essentially stand on two of them and hover, while this one swings up and creates a distortion in front of it, allowing the craft to slide forward..."

To capitalize on the purported extraterrestrial activity the Nevada Commission on Tourism sought to rename the highway. Locals suggested the Extraterrestrial Alien Highway. But this was a bridge too far, too audacious perhaps. State Officials came together, tossed it around a while and settled on something far less poignant. The "Extraterrestrial Highway." I wasn't there for the fanfare, the soiree.

For some, the press-agentry was just the start. But, as if flying-saucery, ufology had some kind of scientific legitimacy, some locals were guilelessly irked, jibbed: kooks, crazy colourful people of all manner clamouring into our town, spoiling serious scientific study, they would holler. But, one local, a straight-talking fella, I've been back and forth on the UFO thing, I've seen fantastic lights. Great glowing orbs. Stupendous UFOs – but you know half the US Army is just over yonder, over that hilltop. They're up night and day, those son-of-a-bitches, turn night into day with their goddamn fan-dangle contraptions.

The military is there, so is the CIA. A dusty unmarked road leads to the front gate of Area 51. It's protected off course, a chain link fence, a boom gate, and those signs we spoke about. Don't be fooled, the facility is under closer guard - they are watching. The area surrounding the base is permanently off-limits to both civilian and normal military air traffic. Security clearances are checked regularly. Beyond the gate, CCTV sentries gyrate punctiliously.

On distant hilltops, with the sun right, one can just make out the trucks, chrome body parts and glass, shimmering, giving up their lair. Government contractors, in white Ford Raptors, armed with orders. Locals say the base knows every desert tortoise and jackrabbit that hops the fence. Others claim of embedded sensors in the approaching road. They are right.

The amount of information the government has been willing to provide has generally been trifling. Cameras and weaponry are strictly prohibited. Even military pilots training in the area risk disciplinary action should they stray into the exclusionary zone, the "box", surrounding Groom's airspace. On most early mornings, eagle-eyed visitors can spot strange lights in the sky moving up and down. These are actually the semi-secret contract commuter airline plans using the call-sign "Janet" that transports workers from Las Vegas's McCarran Airport to the base.

The government did in fact officially acknowledge the existence of Area 51, suggesting that the area served a far less remarkable purpose. In 2013, the National Security Archive at the George Washington University obtained through the Freedom of Information a formerly classified CIA document that chronicled the history of the U-2, a high-altitude reconnaissance aircraft. After the U-2 was put into service in 1956, Area 51 was used to develop other aircraft, including the A-12 reconnaissance plane and the stealth fighter F-117 Nighthawk.

Until recently, satellite imagery of the installation was censored. As of 2018, Area 51 is visible on Google Maps. Shrewdly, I mean, inanely, the United States Geological Survey topographic map still shows only the existence of a century and a half old silver and lead mine. Groom Mine ceased operations in the '50s. Half a century later, under eminent domain, the Government seized it from its owners, the Sheahan family. Plenty of landowners have fought governments over property appropriations. However, the struggle the Sheahan's have endured in their fight to hang on to their mine has been an epic quest of David and Goliath proportions.

The family's remote frontier lifestyle was largely left alone until the early 40s. Their ancestors originally settled on the site more than a century ago, long before Lockheed and the CIA came down. Founded by Patrick Sheahan in 1889, the Sheahan family worked the mine for decades, extracting silver, lead, zinc, and copper. Eventually a second generation of the family, also called the mine, home. But once the Atomic Energy Commission moved in nearby, the once-quiet, pristine wilderness was now the forefront of the atomic age, the test site, a place from which the Cold War's nuclear race would start.

The Sheahans' experience with the test site has no extraterrestrial allure. But it began with a different kind of mystery: As the family's story goes, on June 23, 1954, around lunchtime, the heart of the mine, its hand-built ore processing mill was destroyed by what they say was an aerial bombardment. With their extended family gone, Dan and Martha Sheahan battled alone against an inferno that strangely engulfed the mill for nearly three days straight.

An investigation was conducted into the loss of the mill by the Nevada mining giant Basic Magnesium Inc.'s fire chief. It states that due to the high temperature of the inferno, the source of the fire was most likely from an "outside origin," An outside origin, perhaps – human, certainly.

3. Of rubber strips, tinfoil, tough paper and sticks

What goes on inside Area 51 has led to decades of wild speculation. There are, of course, the extraterrestrial conspiracies, galactic tourists tucked away somewhere under imponderable hangers. In mid 1947, there was, indeed, a UFO confrontation.

A United States Army Air Forces balloon crashed at a ranch near Roswell, New Mexico. What followed has been an almost quotidian but no less harrowing idiosyncratic crusade - catalyst for the conspiracy craze and inescapable on television. Subsequent to wide initial interest in the crashed "flying saucer", the defence department was emphatic, it was just a balloon, a conventional weather balloon and interest waned until the 70's. But now, that was no weather balloon, said ufologists. One or more extraterrestrial spacecraft had crash-landed, the occupants, extraterrestrials, had been recovered.

On June 14, 1947, William Brazel, a foreman working on the Foster homestead, noticed clusters of debris approximately 30 miles north of Roswell, New Mexico. This date, or "about three weeks" before July 8, appeared in later stories featuring Brazel, but the initial press release from the Roswell Army Air Field said the find was "sometime last week", suggesting Brazel found the debris in early July. Brazel told the *Roswell Daily Record* that he and his son saw a "large area of bright wreckage made up of rubber strips, tinfoil, a rather tough paper and sticks." He paid little attention to it but returned on July 4 with his son, wife and daughter to gather up the material. Some accounts have described Brazel as having gathered some of the material earlier, rolling it together and stashing it under some brush.

The next day, Brazel heard reports about "flying discs" and wondered if that was what he had gathered up. On July 7, Brazel saw Sheriff Wilcox and "whispered kinda confidential like" that he may have found a flying disc. Another account quotes Wilcox as saying Brazel reported the object on July 6.

Wilcox called Roswell Army Air Field Major Jesse Marcel and a "man in plainclothes" accompanied Brazel back to the ranch where more pieces were picked up. "We spent a couple of hours Monday afternoon, July 7, looking for any more parts of the weather device", said Marcel. "We found a few more patches of tinfoil and rubber."

On July 8, 1947, Roswell Army Air Field public information officer Walter Haut issued a press release stating that personnel from the field's 509th Operations Group had recovered a "flying disc", which had crashed on a ranch near Roswell. As described in the July 9, 1947 edition of the *Roswell*

Daily Record,

> *The balloon which held it up, if that was how it worked, must have been 12 feet long, [Brazel] felt, measuring the distance by the size of the room in which he sat. The rubber was smoky grey in colour and scattered over an area about 200 yards in diameter. When the debris was gathered up, the tinfoil, paper, tape, and sticks made a bundle about three feet long and 7 or 8 inches thick, while the rubber made a bundle about 18 or 20 inches long and about 8 inches thick. In all, he estimated, the entire lot would have weighed maybe five pounds.*

> *There was no sign of any metal in the area which might have been used for an engine, and no sign of any propellers of any kind, although at least one paper fin had been glued onto some of the tinfoil. There were no words to be found anywhere on the instrument, although there were letters on some of the parts. Considerable Scotch tape and some tape with flowers printed upon it had been used in the construction. No strings or wires were to be found but there were some eyelets in the paper to indicate that some sort of attachment may have been used.*

A telex sent to a FBI office from the Fort Worth, Texas office quoted a Major from the Eighth Air Force (also based in Fort Worth at Carswell Air Force

Base) on July 8, 1947 as saying that "The disc is hexagonal in shape and was suspended from a balloon [sic] by cable, which balloon [sic] was approximately twenty feet in diameter. Major Curtan further advises [sic] that the object found resembles a high-altitude weather balloon with a radar reflector, but that telephonic conversation between their office and Wright field had not borne out this belief." Early on Tuesday, July 8, the RAAF issued a press release, which was immediately picked up by numerous news outlets:

> *The many rumours regarding the flying disc became a reality yesterday when the intelligence office of the 509th Bomb group of the Eighth Air Force, Roswell Army Air Field, was fortunate enough to gain possession of a disc through the cooperation of one of the local ranchers and the sheriff's office of Chaves County.*
>
> *The flying object landed on a ranch near Roswell sometime last week. Not having phone facilities, the rancher stored the disc until such time as he was able to contact the sheriff's office, who in turn notified Maj. Jesse A. Marcel of the 509th Bomb Group Intelligence Office. Action was immediately taken, and the disc was picked up at the rancher's home. It was inspected at the Roswell Army Air Field and subsequently loaned by Major Marcel to higher headquarters.*

Colonel William H. Blanchard, commanding officer of the 509th, contacted General Roger M. Ramey of the Eighth Air Force in Fort Worth, Texas, and Ramey ordered the object be flown to Fort Worth Army Air Field. At the base, Warrant Officer Irving Newton confirmed Ramey's preliminary opinion, identifying the object as being a weather balloon and its "kite", a nickname for a radar reflector used to track the balloons from the ground. Another news release was issued, this time from the Fort Worth base, describing the object as being a "weather balloon."

As far as social costs go, to avoid them, the military decided to conceal the true purpose of the crashed device – a nuclear test monitoring device. Instead they informed the public that the crash was of a weather balloon. Later that day, the press reported that Commanding General of the Eighth Air Force Roger Ramey had stated that a weather balloon was recovered by the RAAF personnel. A press conference was held, featuring debris (foil, rubber and wood) said to be from the crashed object, which matched the weather balloon description. Historian Robert Goldberg wrote that the intended effect was achieved: "the story died the next day."

Between 1978 and the early 1990s, UFO researchers interviewed several hundred people who claimed to have had a connection with the events at Roswell. Hundreds of documents were obtained via Freedom of Information Act requests, along with other documents such as Majestic 12 that were supposedly leaked by insiders. Their conclusions were that at least one extraterrestrial spacecraft crashed near Roswell, extraterrestrial bodies had been recovered, and a government cover-up of the incident had taken place.

Over the years, books, articles, and television specials brought the 1947 incident notoriety. By the mid-1990s, public polls revealed that the majority of people interviewed believed that extraterrestrials had indeed visited Earth, and that extraterrestrials had landed at Roswell, but that all the relevant information was being kept secret by the US government.

According to anthropologists, the Roswell Story was the prime example of how a discourse moved from the fringes to the mainstream according to the prevailing zeitgeist: public preoccupation in the 1980s with "conspiracy, cover-up and repression" aligned well with the Roswell narratives as told in the "sensational books" which were being published. Another problem - out of many hundreds of people were interviewed by the various researchers, but critics point out that only a few of these people claimed to have actually seen debris or extraterrestrials. Most witnesses were repeating the claims of others.

An extraterrestrial flying object made out of rubber strips, tinfoil, a rather tough paper and sticks. I have to whisper kinda confidential like, if only they found that damn propeller thing, y'all woulda show more respect now if only we found that damn propeller. Clearly, we are unable to understand the means of other *spices* except by generalizing from the human experience. We are permanently trapped in an anthropocentric predicament. To make meaning of the extraterrestrial we seem to rely upon the human analogy.

4. Perverse, outlandish developments

We all believe in things that are obviously untrue, even demonstrably false. In our wish to believe in someone, a thing, a political administration, we accept propagated falsehoods - in the case of Governments, large swaths of the population can buy into. But the collective delusion is not new, nor is it the sole province of any one political group. For example, many believe, counter to scientific consensus, that genetically modified foods are poisonous, and that vaccines cause autism.

The situation is vexing because it seems so very easy to disentangle. The truth should be obvious if we just look for it, right? But this line of thinking leads to explanations of the hoodwinked masses that amount to little more than disparagement; ridiculed and called crackpots and crazy. This relieves us of certain discomforts, but it's misguided.

On our own, we're are not always able to separate what's fact and what's not. Ignorance is our natural state; it is a product of the way our mind works. What really sets us apart is not our individual mental capacity. Our success is our ability to cooperate, pursue complex goals by dividing cognitive chores. Hunting, trade, agriculture, manufacturing — all that has been truly species changing endeavours.

The corollary is of course also true - we have trouble believing the truth. Of the many forms of faulty thinking that have been identified, confirmation bias, the tendency people have to embrace information that supports their beliefs and reject information that contradicts them is among the best understood. Facts don't always change our minds. Once formed, impressions are remarkably perseverant. Any graduate student in a psychology course will tell you, reasonable-seeming people will often be totally irrational.

The most dramatic early UFO encounter occurred in 1897 Texas, when E.E. Haydon, a newspaper reporter for the Dallas Morning News, described an amazing encounter complete with a crashed spacecraft, dozens of eyewitnesses, a recovered dead Martian body, and metallic wreckage (50 years later a nearly identical story would circulate about a crash in the neighbouring state of New Mexico). The fantastic tale unravelled when researchers could find no eyewitnesses to support Haydon's story, and nothing of the extraterrestrial or the "several tons" of mysterious spacecraft wreckage was ever found. It turned out that Haydon had made the whole story up as a publicity stunt to attract tourists.

So, the explanation, experimental aircraft fly over Area 51 doesn't quite gel. There are those convinced that what they've seen defies terrestrial creation. "I don't know if I believe in UFOs or not but I think at this point, with all the things I've seen and the people

I've talked to, there's got to be something out there that's not us," says, a middle-aged Rachel wife and mother, employed full-time to investigate UFO phenomena.

"I've been seeing UFOs since the Fifties, but the most frightening incident, occurred in 1993, about five miles out of Rachel. I noticed three lights bobbing in the air about 100 yards away, as if they were bobbing on water. There were three UFOS, each about 100ft across, and they had three huge globes of light underneath them. I pulled the car over to take a picture, and when I turned my lights out, all of their lights went out," she says. "When I turned my lights back on, all of theirs went back on - but by then they had moved about five miles to the south. That was the first time in my life that it occurred to me that if I could see them, they could see me. It took me about 30 minutes to make the 70 miles home."

Her fear rekindled the memory of another mysterious phenomenon, she says. Her family used to farm a million-acre ranch, 100 miles across the desert from Rachel. One morning, the cowboys came up to the farmhouse, badly shaken. "They told us that they were already packed and leaving because what they'd seen had scared them so badly," she says. It was a dead bull. "At first my dad thought it had been struck by lightning - until we saw everything that had been done to it."

Its sexual organs had been removed. There were perfectly round holes in all of the joints and in the ear and the lip. It had been drained of blood, and yet there were no bloodstains, either on its body or in the immediate vicinity. "We had an inspector come from Carson City and put a Geiger counter over it and it was radioactive. The coyotes wouldn't eat it." It strikes me interesting that visiting extraterrestrials seem to show a wholesome percolative for sexual genitalia. This may because most composite descriptions of our visitors are said to be missing external human organs, noses, ears and sex organs.

And there have been numerous abductions. Kidnappings in extraterrestrial-spaceships, medical examinations with proclivities for genitalia, sometimes getting past first base: salacious sexual encounters with mysterious tell-tale signs a forensics delight. One story of an abduction took place in 1957 centring around Antônio Villas Boas, a farmer from rural Brazil.

According to Villas Boas, he was ploughing fields with his tractor when he was taken against his will by a group of extraterrestrials. On their spaceship he was put in a room. He says he became ill, the effect of a gas belched out through outlets around the vacant room. Then a very attractive female, naked, with long platinum-blonde hair, fire-red pubic hair and deep-blue cat eyes, came to him and forced him to have intercourse. Suffice to say, the poor fellow was given no chance to dither. Devious extraterrestrials had tapped into the human mind, they understood the Freudian psyche.

Sexuality, anyone's failing. And sex, a prime motivator and a common denominator. Even, or perhaps especially, the most prudent, puritanical struggle greatly against sexual expression. Fantasies conjure up all kinds of perverse and outlandish scenarios. Villas Boas' ideas of erotica, notwithstanding, the scenarios for sexual fantasies vary greatly. Not just between individuals, but by personal desires and experiences ranging from the mundane to the bizarre. Alien eroticism, probably a fetish acceptable – but surly, the physical, incompatible.

Our bits and bobs are likely to be totally different, having developed along unique evolutionary lines and circumstances. For one thing, it's unclear to me whether the familiar gender binary would be replicated in an extraterrestrial. Two-gender biology may be unlikely on other planets; it doesn't even always exist on this planet.

In the beginning of Disney's "Finding Nemo", a father clownfish is left to care for his one remaining egg, which grows up to be Nemo, after the mother was eaten by a barracuda. If this were real life, though, Nemo wouldn't be without a mother for long. Nemo's dad would just change his sex to become a mother. That's because clownfish, like many plants and animals, are hermaphrodites. So, you see, the separate male and female sexes aren't even universal a rule in our oceans, let alone others. Hermaphrodites can essentially have sex with themselves and without another.

Hermaphroditism happens a few different ways in nature. Simultaneous hermaphrodites, snails, for example, are born with both male and female sex organs, so any two members of the species can usually mate, or even fertilize themselves. There are also what are known as sequential hermaphrodites, which is an organism that's born with one set of sex organs but can change them at some point in its life. If it's born as a male and switches to female, that's called protandry; the reverse, and it's called protogyny.

It's sometimes edifying to note that concepts from evolutionarily biology conjoined with Kantian and Nietzschean based assessment demonstrate that our human concepts and perspectives are hopelessly Earthen.

5. Our biased minds

I have come to a serious realization that objectivity is a myth, at best a rarity. I think it was a romantic idea from the very beginning, that a person can look at a fact and see it for what it is. Facts are facts. They can be numbers, they can be things, objects. They should be easy enough to appreciate and accept as they are. In fact, they may be to the human mind, but hardly to the human person.

For a long time, I must have become somewhat lazy, preferring to take the path of least resistance, especially with what we call facts, knowledge, and truth. It had become easy to believe that what I see, hear and learn are facts, knowledge and truth – and anything to the contrary is false. After all, I have had extensive experience, having lived all of four decades and, perhaps, an extraordinary exposure to people, events and places that the majority of people don't have. I always had good grades in subjects I wanted to study, and a quick, instinctive or intuitive grasp of what's what in life. Also, I had reasonable courage to face hard truths, especially my shortcomings.

Because I write, and more importantly, I read, I am always engaged with the unlimited spectrum of human imagination and artistry. Many writers can have such unimaginable creativity, snatching thought images from nowhere and everywhere, that they are making life so enthralling and thrilling to those who read them. Many more have such gift with words that I am stunned by how they manipulate language from just being informative to being simply awesome. These writers who have such intelligence and profound insights, these writers who use words like music and dance, they make up for everything else.

On the evening of October 30, 1938, radio listeners across the U.S. heard a startling report of mysterious creatures and terrifying war machines moving toward New York City. Orson Welles announced to audiences in a chilling radio performance that Martians were invading New Jersey. But the so-called news was fake – it was the dramatization of the H.G. Wells science-fiction classic, "The War of the Worlds," and was part of a weekly series of dramatic broadcasts created in collaboration with the Mercury Theatre on the Air for CBS, according to the programme.

During the radio transmission, an actor posing as a news announcer interrupted a scheduled music performance. With a tone of rising alarm, he described telescope observations of "three explosions" on Mars, then brought in on-the-scene reporting from Grover's Mill, a town near Princeton, New Jersey. As the drama unfolded, performers posing as witnesses described unidentified flying objects (UFOs) and "strange creatures" firing a futuristic heat ray that had killed dozens of people. "Thousands of listeners rushed from their homes in New York and New Jersey, many with towels across their faces to protect themselves from the 'gas' which the invader was supposed to be spewing forth," the Daily News reported the next day.

Not long after the factious War, before World War II, in the pioneer years of ships of the air, the dirigible – large intercontinental cigar shaped balloons, blimps, took to cruising the skies. Today, blimps are best known as advertising vehicles and we rarely give them a second thought. Goodyear, for example, began using blimps to advertise their brand as early as 1925. But blimps have also played an important role in the armed forces of many countries; the U.S. Navy's lighter-than-air program made extensive use of blimps, primarily in anti-submarine and reconnaissance roles, from the 1920s through the 1950s.

Just how these ships are perceived by some, indeed how most unusual objects are perceived when they are flying high against the sun, or when they're reflecting scattered light in the early evening, varies, understandably from time to time from person to person. We tend to notice things that are already primed in memory, repeated frequently, such as for example if stories of UFO sightings have recently been in high circulation. A simple rule of our brain, one of a number of cognitive biases exists for reasons primarily to save our brains time and energy, that it's more likely to notice things that are related to things that's recently been stored in memory.

Object seen in the sky, especially in poor light, are difficult to identify at first glance – the limitations of human perception genuinely defied. Our sense of sight is the most used, most often relied upon to experience and conceive the world around us. It gives us colour, value, texture, pattern, line, shape and space. But even in the realm of visual experience it is limited – limited by range, detail, clarity, and depth. It's easy for our eyes to play tricks on the mind.

There are of course other biases - we wouldn't survive without them. Evolutionary bias has helped, continue to help resolve a number of important problems. Problems such as information overload, situations that lack meaning, in circumstances where we need to act with hast, and how to know what needs to be remembered and what not.

To deal with the first problem, when we are bombarded with too much information - we have no choice but to filter. Our brain uses a few simple tricks to pick out the bits of information that are most likely going to be useful in some way. As mentioned, we notice things that are already primed. As well, our brains tend to boost the importance of things that are unusual and surprising. Alternatively, we tend to skip over information that we think is ordinary, expected. We are drawn to details that confirm our own beliefs. As is the corollary: we tend to ignore details that contradicts our beliefs we hold dear. And, we notice when things have changed. Consider a distant light, it stands out more when it starts to blink.

The world is more complex than it ever has been before - this is true by almost any measure. Not only is the rate of change increasing, technological advancement, the rate of knowledge creation, and there is no doubt that global communication systems are becoming more interconnected, the number of people plugging into these complex networks is increasing. We are reaching a number of critical tipping points in human history that are drawing our attention to a reality that our world is (and always was) made up of highly interdependent and deeply connected complex systems. So, consequently, perhaps inevitably, we end up only seeing a tiny sliver.

In this narrow sliver stream of information, we connect the dots, fill in the gaps with what we already think we know. We find stories and patterns even in sparse data, but a great anxiety grows inside us – we now know we'll never have the luxury of having the full story. We fill in characteristics from stereotypes, generalities, and histories. We imagine things and people we're familiar with, fond of, as better than things and people we aren't familiar with, fond of. We project our current mindset and assumptions onto the past and our future selves.

Without our ability to act quickly in the face of uncertainty, we surely would have perished as a species a long time ago. With every emerging situation, a piece of new information, we need to do our best to calibrate our ability to affect the situation, apply it to decisions, simulate the future, predict what might happen in the next iteration. But we value those more in the present and relate more to stories of specific individuals than anonymous individuals. The views of the local perish are that much more reliable.

What should we remember? There's just too much information. We can only afford to keep around what we think will prove useful in the future. It's a juggling act, constant bets and trade-offs around what we should try to remember and what we should let go. Thus, we prefer generalizations over specifics, they take up less space. When there many irreducible details, we pick and save standouts, and discard the others. What we save here is self-reinforcing. We edit and reinforce some memories after the fact. We discard specifics to form generalities. Of course, we see unidentified flying objects, our brain has "fill in" the missing information, mislead us with unreliable memories

Sightings of three lights in the night sky are reported as appearing as a triangular spacecraft. The fact is that any three lights in the sky, whether connected or not, will form a triangle if you assume (without evidence) that each of those lights are fixed at the ends of three points. Had a witness seen four lights he or she would have assumed it was a rectangular-shaped object in the night sky above him; our brains sometimes make connections where none exist.

The way we see the world is a perception on a number of levels. While we often think of the reality we observe as being objective, the truth is actually that the objective and the subjective very much overlap in how we view things and how we feel about them. Everything that we call reality is something we have developed a subjective emotional response to. When we look out at the world, we're not just seeing what's there. Our judgment of our observation is also being influenced by the feelings we've developed towards them over time.

Quantum mechanics has taught us that our reality may be an illusion, that at the quantum level, reality does not even exist if we're not looking at it. More so, life is an illusion, at least on a quantum level. Everything we take for granted as reality is, in fact, an illusion of sorts.

Pragmatically, perception is created by our brain; from what's actually being captured by our eye. For one thing light receptors on the surface of the retina are not smoothly distributed, and there is a blind spot roughly in the centre. If our brain didn't modify what the eye was capturing, we would see things quite differently. So, the magic of the brain is it's capable to patch them up and create a perception of a smooth view. How does the brain do it? It patches up from our experience of how a view supposed to be. It is entirely feasible that reality does not exist independently of us the observer.

So, when twelve helium balloons escaped an engagement party held for a teacher at the Milestone School in Mount Vernon, in 2010, hundreds of people in Manhattan's Chelsea neighbourhood saw a cluster of silvery, shiny lights glittering from above. Naturally, initial descriptions of the supposed UFO varied wildly:

Some folks reported seeing one large, slow-moving object full of lights, while others say they saw nearly a half-dozen entities. Extraterrestrial spacecraft was of course a popular theory, though most New Yorkers seemed to take the lights in stride. Officials said that the objects were not detected as any security threat, and FAA spokesman said that the UFO did not appear on radar: "We re-ran radar to see if there was anything there that we can't account for but there is nothing in the area."

The term "UFO" automatically triggers derision in most quarters of polite society. People seeing cigar shaped UFOs, obviously inspired by dirigible balloons. Mysterious UFO sightings may go hand-in-hand with a natural weather phenomenon known as sprites flashes high in the atmosphere triggered by thunderstorms. Unusual cloud formations and lightning are close contenders. A footage of a giant halo in an overcast sky over Moscow surfaced on YouTube a couple of years ago. The video had everything needed to ignite UFO rumours. It's grainy. At one point, a dark pointy object appears to bolt out of the ring. There's even a panicked-sounding Russian radio broadcast in the background. Indeed, I think that any UFO researcher would tell you that 98 per cent of sightings that happen are very easily explainable.

But modern UFO mythology began with the Kenneth Arnold UFO sighting in 1947 and he said he saw discs. Once that inspired Hollywood, they showed us plenty of disc shaped extraterrestrial craft and thoroughly established the idea in the popular imagination. The term "Flying Saucer" can be traced back to June 24, 1947, and a private pilot named Kenneth Arnold. Arnold was flying past Mt. Rainier in Washington State, and noticed a stack of something that looked like saucers. He reported what he saw, and the term he used got corrupted into "Flying Saucers". And what he really saw were lenticular clouds. Quite common around solitary mountain peaks. And they really do look spectacular.

Why an extraterrestrial race would flit about at night with your little "saucer" all lit up like a Christmas tree - UFO sightings go back some 4000 years. But it's only been in the past century or so that anybody assumed that unknown lights or objects in the sky were visitors from other planets.

Several of the planets had been noticed for millennia but were not thought of as places where other living creatures might reside. In Egypt for example, according to the disputed Tulli Papyrus, the scribes of the pharaoh Thutmose III reported that "fiery disks" were encountered floating over the skies. And, in 74 BC, according to Plutarch, a Roman army commanded by Lucullus was about to begin a battle with Mithridates VI of Pontus when "all on a sudden, the sky burst asunder, and a huge, flame-like body was seen to fall between the two armies.

In shape, it was most like a wine-jar, and in colour, like molten silver." Plutarch reports the shape of the object as like a wine-jar (pithos.) The apparently silvery object was reported by both armies.

In the Holy Roman Empire, 1561, residents of Nuremberg saw what they described as an aerial battle, followed by the appearance of a large black triangular object and then a large crash outside of the city. The broadsheet claims that witnesses observed hundreds of spheres, cylinders and other odd-shaped objects that moved erratically overhead.

In Japan, in 1803 local fishermen reportedly saw a vessel drifting in close-by waters. They say when they investigated it, "a beautiful young woman" they described as having red and white hair and dressed in strange clothes appeared. The fishermen claim she held a square box "that no one was allowed to touch" and she spoke to them in a language they never heard before. Some UFO believers think this story was a credible document of a close encounter of the third kind in Japan. Historians and Ethnologists consider it to be folklore.

In 1917, thousands of people observed the sun gyrate and descend. This was later reinterpreted by Jacques Vallée, Joaquim Fernandes and Fina d'Armada as a possible UFO sighting, but not recognized as such due to cultural differences.

The putative propulsion method for "alien spacecraft" is usually left as "unknown" or drawn on science-fiction references along the lines of gravo-magnetic systems which somehow tap into the Earth's magnetic field. Antimatter reactors and Hyperdrive are popular too. How these systems aid craft journey between solar systems is never explained. But many enthusiasts postulate a "mother ship." A sort of interstellar aircraft carrier which disgorges the little "saucers" on arrival at the destination. Why expend the resources to construct a huge spaceship and perhaps dozens of other smaller craft, and a large crew, for the purpose of flitting around the target planet with no contact what soever?

At least with science fiction, you know it's a scam. Who can forget Star Trek's Warp Drive. surely the most famous way to get you to a distant star. The idea, not exactly a simple explanation - if you combine matter and antimatter fused with some Dilithium, you can create a subspace bubble that exists outside the normal fabric of space–time. Star

Wars struck on the technology of Hyperdrive, a system maintained—if you follow the legendary Wookiee warrior, Chewbacca's model—by banging on the ship's interior plating until, finally, you go fast. However, those with an engineering nonce will be comfortable with the explanation that this involves collecting gamma radiation, fusing it in a hyperdrive motivator, and maintaining a stable corridor of space with a null quantum field generator.

My favourite, however, is the Infinite Improbability Drive found in "The Hitchhiker's Guide to the Galaxy." In what's beating within Zaphod Beeblebrox's commandeered ship Heart of Gold, the Infinite Improbability Drive is one of the more purely mathematical systems of faster-than-light travel, making quantum calculations determining the least likely point in space and then suddenly sending you there.

6. We've got little green men on the brain

Little green men with elongated limbs and saucer-like eyes, pop-culture short hand that can mean only one thing: extraterrestrial life. This universal description of extraterrestrial beings — which are usually mischievous or even downright malevolent — has endured as a staple of innumerable solemn documentaries, science-fiction vocabulary, the poster face for extraterrestrials, most often from Mars.

But where did the idea of the diminutive, verdant, otherworldly intruders come from, and how did it come to be so widely accepted as an archetypal example to most would-be visitors from afar? Before its more modern application to extraterrestrials, little green men were commonly used to describe various supernatural beings in old legends and folklore and in later fairy tales and children's books such as goblins.

The trope may actually predate both science fiction, and the first sighting of UFOs itself, hearkening back to a 12th-century English legend known as "The Green Children of Woolpit." One day at harvest time, according to William of Newburgh, a 12th century British writer, the villagers of Woolpit discovered two children, a brother and sister, beside one of the wolf pits that gave the village its name. Their skin was green, they spoke an unknown language, and their clothing was unfamiliar. The children were taken to the home of Richard de Calne, a prominent town squire.

As the story goes, the Lamprey pair refused all food for several days until they came across some raw broad beans, which they consumed eagerly. The children gradually adapted to normal food and in time lost their green colour. The boy, who appeared to be the younger of the two, became sickly and died shortly after he and his sister were baptised.

After learning to speak English, the children – the surviving girl explained that they came from a land where the Sun never shone and the light similar to twilight. The children called their home St Martin's Land; adding that everything there was green in colour. According to William of Newburgh, the children were unable to account for their arrival in Woolpit; they had been herding their father's cattle when they heard a loud noise (the bells of Bury St Edmunds) and suddenly found themselves by the wolf pit where they were found.

Ralph says that they had become lost when they followed the cattle into a cave and, after being guided by the sound of bells, eventually emerged into our land. According to Ralph of Coggeshall, another writer, the girl was employed for many years as a servant in Richard de Calne's household, where she was considered to be "very wanton and impudent".

The girl was given the name "Agnes" and that she married a royal official named Richard Barre.

The first recorded instance of the phrase "little green men", though specifically, the title is "Small green men in Mayaya" was a story from Harold Lawlor and dates back to 1946. Frederic Brown's popular science-fiction novel, "Martians, Go Home" (E.P. Dutton, 1955) reinforced the idea of small, green-skinned extraterrestrial invaders that are more irritating than dangerous. Rather than engaging Earth's armies in deadly battles for global domination, Brown's little green men preferred to spend their time playing annoying and embarrassing pranks.

These examples illustrate that use of little green men was already deeply engrained in English vernacular long before the flying saucer era, used for a variety of supernatural, imaginary, or mythical beings. It also seems to have easily extended beyond the imaginary to real people, such as the reference to small actors in the Wizard of Oz or camouflaged Japanese soldiers.

Similarly, when flying saucers came along in 1947, with subsequent speculation about extraterrestrial origins, the term naturally and quickly attached itself to the modern age equivalent. It is also clear that by the early 1950s, the term was already commonly used as a sarcastic reference to the occupants of flying saucers. By 1954, the image of little green men had become inscribed in the public's collective consciousness.

These stories show that even in the past the idea of extraterrestrials being green was not an uncommon thought and worked its way into popular culture. Shows such as the Flintstones and other old cartoons featured extraterrestrials who were green and Disney's Toy Story extraterrestrials have become an icon recognizable by many.

Some take a single facet of humanity and amplify it – perhaps a distorted representation of ourselves, a puckishness and a fondness for troublemaking extraterrestrial Ninjas, or childlike innocence and wonder, such as E.T. from the film "E.T. the Extraterrestrial," Uncle Martin in "My Favourite Martian." Others represent a darker side of humanity: Picture the ruthless, shape-shifting creatures in the "Alien" movie series, or the marauding Klingons from "Star Trek."

Why humanity specifically grasped onto this portrayal of extraterrestrials is partly due to the things which we regard as most important, i.e. cognitive sophistication, large brains, intelligence, tool making, that are perhaps evolutionary convergence is completely ubiquitous. But over the passage of the years the notion of little green men has implied a certain, a kind of pathology.

In 1923, a serialized romance, When Hearts Command by Elizabeth York Miller, which appeared in newspapers such as the Chicago Tribune and Washington Post, has a former mental patient who still sees "little green men" and who simultaneously comments that a fellow patient "conversed with the inhabitants of Mars".

Another instance, in a newspaper column from 1936 sarcastically discussing doctors and their medical advice, saying these are the same people who have breakdowns in middle age and start hallucinating "a little green man with big ears". Syndicated columnist Sydney J. Harris used "little green man" in 1948 as a child's imaginary friend while condemning the age-old tradition of frightening children with stories of "boogeymen."

Keith E. Stanovich, in his wonderful text, How to Think Straight About Psychology discusses and compares scientific theory with a layman's interpretation of theory. He writes that scientific theories are larger conceptual structures informed by bodies of data, while a layman's theory - simple, unconnected, an unverified hypothesis, a guess like common sense, one "theory" is as good as the other. Interestingly, he suggests that scientific Theory must also meet the falsifiability criterion.

Making sure theories are falsifiable have implications for actual events in the natural world. These criteria include methods of evaluating new evidence mindful that any theory must always include the possibility that the data will falsify the theory. Dis-conforming evidence often gives us more information than a confirmation - with a universal generalization, one disconfirmation is all you need. Humans are prone to confirmation bias, that we need the scientific method to counteract it.

In the second chapter, Falsifiability: How to Foil Little Green Men in the Head, Stanovich delves deeper into his third characteristic of science: Scientists deal with solvable problems. To define "solvable problems" in this context, we must start with two critical concepts: first, what are the defining characteristics of a scientific theory, and second, what does it mean to be falsifiable?

Scientific theories must always be stated in such a way that the predictions derived from them could potentially be shown to be false. This principle is known as the falsifiability criterion, and it is attributed to the philosopher of science Karl Popper. Popper argued that nothing in science was verifiable (you can't prove anything to be absolutely true) but that all science must be falsifiable (you must be able to prove it false).

Stanovich highlights that good theories go out on a limb and make predictions which might not be true. He discusses two theories that were not science, because they resisted exactly this: Freud's theory and bloodletting (using Benjamin Rush as an example.)

Freud's theory, built on case studies and extensive storytelling did not make prediction, but rather explanations of behaviour after the fact. For example, he mentions the many psychoanalytic explanations for Tourette's syndrome. Tics were a source or erotic pleasure, and therefore the patient did not want to give them up, "a conversion symptom at the anal-sadistic level," symptoms of a "narcissistic character."

> *Sandor Ferenczi, a disciple of Freud who had never seen a patient with Tourette's [italics added by Stanovich] made an equally serious error when he wrote that the frequent facial tics of people with Tourette's were the result of a repressed urge to masturbate"*

The story was similar with bloodletting. Benjamin Rush, a famous American surgeon and patriot, would justify treatment of bloodletting by explaining everything. If a patient died, "The disease was too far gone for the treatment to work" if they recovered, well then, "the treatment worked!"

The key for me here is that science must be in the language and spirit of prediction. Scientific theories must both explain existing facts and guide the search for new facts. In this search, theories must make real predictions that can be proved wrong.

Stanovich does a good job finding a middle ground between Popper and his students like Imre Lakatos and Paul Feyerabendian, who characterized scientists from a much more sociological point of view. He ends that section by citing a light-hearted ribbing from psychologist Ray Nickerson that science proceeds through falsification, not because individual scientists enjoy being wrong, but because they enjoy showing that other scientists' theories are wrong.

Which reminds me of this delightfully ranty post from Peter Watts about those leaked emails in Climategate.

> *Science doesn't work despite scientists being asses. Science works, to at least some extent, because scientists are asses. Bickering and backstabbing are essential elements of the process. Haven't any of these guys ever heard of "peer review"?*
>
> *There's this myth in wide circulation: rational, emotionless Vulcans in white coats, plumbing the secrets of the universe, their Scientific Methods unsullied by bias or emotionalism. Most people know it's a myth, of course; they subscribe to a more nuanced view in which scientists are as petty and vain and human as anyone (and as egotistical as any therapist or financier), people who use scientific methodology to tamp down their*

human imperfections and manage some approximation of objectivity.

But that's a myth too. The fact is, we are all humans; and humans come with dogma as standard equipment. We can no more shake off our biases than Liz Cheney could pay a compliment to Barack Obama. The best we can do— the best science can do— is make sure that at least, we get to choose among competing biases.

7. In essence, Mr. Hubble reveals we are not alone

"Words are like harpoons," famous astrophysicist and cosmologist Fred Hoyle said in an interview of 1995. "Once they go in, they are very hard to pull out." He referred to the term "big bang," which he had coined nearly half a century earlier for the initial state of the universe without believing, neither then, nor later, that there had ever been such an event.

The name had indeed stuck like a harpoon, and that in spite of many people's dissatisfaction with such an undignified label for the grandest and most mysterious event in the history of the universe, the ultimate beginning of everything. And, as if that irony were not perverse enough, a Belgian Roman Catholic priest, physicist and astronomer, Monsignor Georges Lemaître provided the first definitive formulation of the idea of a theory of the origin of the universe, which Lemaître himself called his "hypothesis of the primeval atom" or the "Cosmic Egg."

On 28 March 1949 he gave a talk on his favoured "continual creation" theory to BBC's Third Programme which shortly thereafter was reproduced in The Listener, the widely circulated BBC magazine. He emphasized the contrast between the Steady State theory and "the hypothesis that all matter of the universe was created in one big bang at a particular time in the remote past", which as I've already mentioned he found to be "irrational" and outside science. Less than a year later he gave a series of five broadcasts on the BBC which again were printed in The Listener and also in the form of the best-selling book, The Nature of the Universe. With Hoyle's radio lectures of 1949 – 1950 the term "Big Bang" made its entry into 20th century cosmological vernacular.

But twenty-five years earlier most astronomers believed that our whole universe consisted of just one galaxy, our own Milky Way. Before the advent of electric lights, everybody on Earth had an unobstructed view of the night sky. The enormous milky band of stars crossing it was impossible to miss. Ancient peoples gave different names to the cloud-like structure of our galaxy, but our modern version derives from the Greeks, who had a myth about the infant Hercules being brought to the goddess Hera, who nursed him while she was asleep. When she awoke and pulled away, her breast milk spilled across the heavens.

For thousands of years Man had observed strange patches of light known as Nebulae laying within the Milky Way. In time, we came to learn that lurking in the heart of our galaxy is a hungry behemoth, a gigantic black hole with the weight equal to about 4 million times the mass of the Sun. And, imagine discovering that your living room, which you've seen a million times before, contained a previously unnoticed elephant. That's more or less what happened to scientists in 2010 when they uncovered gigantic, never-before-seen structures stretching for 25,000 light-years above and below the galaxy.

But in the 1920s, the distant galaxy Andromeda, became part of a "Great Debate" between American astronomers Harlow Shapley and Heber Curtis. Curtis had spotted various Novae in Andromeda and argued instead that Andromeda was a separate, distinct galaxy, another Milky Way, another world. Indeed, as far back as in 964 AD, the Persian astronomer Abd al-Rahman al-Sufi described the galaxy as a "small cloud" in his "Book of Fixed Stars," the first known report of our nearest galactic neighbour.

The Great Debate ensued until Edwin Hubble, a man initially trained in Law, and moved to astronomy, used the largest telescope of his time, the 100-inch Hooker telescope on Mount Wilson in California to show definitively that Andromeda was indeed a distant galaxy. In 1925, he identified a special kind of star known as a Cepheid variable — a star whose characteristics allow for precise measurements of distance — within Andromeda. Because Shapley had previously determined that the Milky Way was only 100,000 light-years across, Hubble's calculations revealed that the fuzzy patch, the Nebulae was too far away to lie within the Milky Way.

Hubble was among the first to recognize that there are a whole universe of galaxies located beyond the boundaries of our Milky Way, Island Universes. This discovery had, instantly, transformed us and our place in the universe. Other, even fainter spiral objects were now probably also distant galaxies, other worlds.

Our galaxy that was once considered the whole, the entire universe just became another amongst, based on current estimates over 500 Billion. So important was this observation that many could not resist the temptation to connect this news with the existence of other life, extraterrestrial life. A search of the Associated Press Archives unearths remarks such as; "In essence, Mr. Hubble reveals we are not alone."

And just five short years later, in 1929 Hubble, by all accounts still the stubborn, ambitious, and sometimes even snobbish young man finds evidence for the idea that the universe is in fact expanding and expanding at an accelerating rate. In the same year, Einstein, his face yellowish, haggard, nervous, and irritable was on the front cover of Time magazine, his accomplishments further recognized - receiving the German Physical Society's first Max Planck Medal. Sometime later, the exact date remains unclear, he is said to have remarked that adjusting general relativity to stop the universe from expanding was his "biggest blunder of his life." If only he knew the half of it.

When Einstein formulated general relativity in 1915, he and his contemporaries believed in a static, that is an unchanging universe. When Einstein found that his equations could easily be solved in such a way as to allow the universe to be expanding now, and to contract in the far future, he added to those equations what he called a cosmological constant, essentially a constant energy density unaffected by any expansion or contraction.

The role of which, was to offset the effect of gravity on the universe as a whole in such a way that the universe would remain static. After Hubble announced his conclusion that the universe was expanding, Einstein wrote that his cosmological constant was "the greatest blunder of my life."

But it was the genius of Einstein to pull back the cloak behind which hid the stuff of the universe. Features that had gone largely unnoticed since man first gazed at the stars. Einstein realized that Newtonian gravity was just an illusion and that it is space itself that is distorted. When we look at a distant star, trusting that it is directly overhead, we never suppose that the path of light coming to us from that star is following the contours of a curved space (and time).

To us, it always seems like it is following a straight line. This understandable, however, parochial view is somewhat analogous to an insect stuck on the surface of our curved planet. It is unable to stand back far enough to see the curvature for what it is. We can't see Einstein's curved universe from the inside. Not only is space-time curved but it's highly likely the universe has no edge.

Hubble's discovery of expanding space, yet with no physical centre, no origin point in three-dimensional space, combined with Einstein's non-Euclidean geometries implied that the cosmos exists in more than the three dimensions we're familiar with in everyday life. That perspective suggests that three-dimensional space could be curved, folded, or warped into a 4th dimension the way that the two-dimensional surface of a balloon is warped into a 3rd dimension. We don't see or feel more dimensions; nevertheless, theoretical physics predicts that they should exist.

As an example, let's imagine that our universe is the 2-dimensional surface of a 3-dimensional sphere, a beachball or a balloon. It is easy to accept that travelling along that surface, just as an Ant crawls over the surface of a balloon, one will never encounter an edge, a boundary that impedes our tour.

This argument, however, is a direct consequence of viewing our 2-dimensional surface as embedded in a 3-dimensional space. In other words, this view arises, because we are looking at the entire balloon, or in effect the universe from the outside. But our minds evolved on the inside of this wily construct, a four-dimensional envelope of space and time. It is beyond our mental-architecture to fully visualise this dimension or any other higher dimension for that matter. Some theories put the number of dimensions at 10, or 11, or 13.

And, like how a 2-dimensional creature (say an extremely, extremely flat worm) sees us, we will only be able to see a part of a 4-dimensional (or higher dimensional) creature's body. In fact, that part of its body that we can see will be 3-dimensional for us, just like how only a 2-dimensional fraction of us would be visible to a 2-dimensional being. Additional insight: Because shadows thrown by a 3-dimensional object appears to be 2-dimensions to us, it's just logical to say that shadows of a 4-dimensional object should appear to be 3-dimensions. An example of the shadow of a 4-dimensional hypercube is called a tesseract.

Fig One.

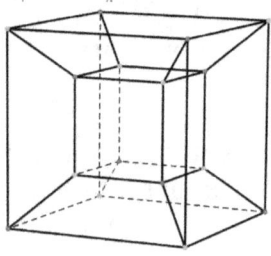

The image shows what the shadow of a tesseract would appear as in a 3-dimensional space. This 3-

dimension shadow consists of two nested cubes, with all their angles connected by lines. In the 4-dimensional space, all the lines of the tesseract would have equal length and all angles right angles. Of course, as 3-dimensional beings, we can't perceive such a thing. In other words, we might actually just be shadows of some 4-dimensional creatures. Or, shadows of some shadows of some 5-dimensional creatures. Maybe those 5-dimensional creatures are also shadows of some 6-dimensional creatures. And maybe those 6-dimensional creatures, too.

extraterrestrials don't necessarily need to be from our dimension. How a 4-dimensional organism interacts with our dimensions and/or influences events in our world is unclear, however, I suspect negligible. Firstly, the 4-dimensional being would likely have mass just as regular beings do. Increasing the dimensionality of space is not known to eliminate the concept of mass. Secondly, if the 4-dimensional being is composed of particles approximately the size of the particles we know of, the probability of a particular 4-dimensional particle being precisely in our 3-dimension plane of existence is very, very small.

Interesting thought, for a 4-dimensional creature, an extraterrestrial, all of us would appear differently from how we appear to each other. To its eyes, all parts of our bodies would be visible all at once: In the same way when we look at a 2-dimensional object, the 4-dimensional extraterrestrial can view us, plus our insides, in all angles at the same time. And, just like how we can easily stick our finger inside a 2-demensional figure, this extraterrestrial can also fiddle with every part of our body without pulling us apart; it can directly interact with our bones without cutting through our skin. So, concealed properties such as bank vaults and prisons are basically defenceless in terms of physical guard against such an extraterrestrial.

General relativity proposes that space and time dimensions are interchangeable and massive objects cause a distortion in space-time. Imagine setting a large body in the centre of a trampoline. The body would press down into the fabric, causing it to dimple. A marble rolled around the edge would spiral inward toward the body, pulled in much the same way that the gravity of a planet pulls at rocks in space. John Archibald Wheeler said it best in Geons, Black Holes, and Quantum Foam, "Space-time tells matter how to move;" and "matter tells space-time how to curve."

Einstein once described himself as a "deeply religious nonbeliever." By such a statement he meant that his worldview was somehow pervaded by an overwhelming and general feeling of religiosity rather than dominated by some specific creedal commitment. Perhaps Einstein's curiosity in the Eucharist might be easier to fathom were we to regard it as a symptom of his abiding and lifelong quest to unravel the eternal enigma of appearance and reality. Relativity theory, in its special and general forms, and, even more iconoclastically, quantum mechanics as we shall see, together caused a complete revolution in human understanding of the physical world, the consequences of which are still to be absorbed into philosophy–and hardly yet into theology.

And any search for other worlds, for extraterrestrial intelligence is all about trying to understand our place in the scheme of things – not merely scientifically, but metaphysically, in terms that inform our worldview. Hence it is no surprise to find that' the knowledge that we are not alone in the universe ... will affect our philosophy, our science, our religion. Of course, Christians have never exactly thought that we were alone in the universe. God, while transcendent, is also immanent: God is with us.

However, some Christians have believed, do believe that humans are the only embodied creatures in creation to be made in God's image. And some atheists love to suggest, it is rarely argued, that if and when one ever detects evidence of an extraterrestrial intelligence ... that evidence will be inconsistent with the existence of God or at least organized religion.

One suspects that some searching for extraterrestrial intelligence enthusiasts look forward to the discovery of extraterrestrial life for just this reason, and that their faith in this actually functions as a bulwark against religion. Of course, unless the search for extraterrestrial programs actually deliver the goods this piece of atheological self-justification will remain another example of what John Polkinghorne calls promissory naturalism.

When In 2014, NASA awarded $1.1M to the Center for Theological Inquiry, an ecumenical research institute in New Jersey, to study "the societal implications of astrobiology" some were enraged. The Freedom From Religion Foundation (FFR), which promotes the division between Church and state, asked NASA to revoke the grant, and threatened to sue. While the FFR stated that their concern was the commingling of government and religious organisations, they also made it clear that they thought the grant was a waste of money. "Science should not concern itself with how its progress will impact faith-based beliefs."

The Big Bang is a theory that attempts to explain the very beginning of time, the beginning of the universe, before which there is no space and no time. Accordingly, the universe sprang into existence as an infinitesimally small, infinitely hot, infinitely dense, energy state - a singularity. The idea that there was no time before the Big Bang isn't new, however. Augustine reached a similar conclusion 1500 years earlier. when, he said, "the world was not, there was no time."

In another beginning, or at least in a variation, according to Genesis, God said, "Let there be light," and there was light. God saw that the light was good, and he separated the light from darkness. The Big Bang on the other hand, predictably, offers a more precise account of light and darkness. Until around 400 million years after the Big Bang, the universe was a very dark place.

As the universe expanded, the hot soup of fundamental particles (such as free protons and electrons) started to cool down. This allowed electrons and protons to pair up and form neutral hydrogen atoms. As free electrons were now bound to protons, light could travel freely since frequent scattering off free electrons was no longer an impediment, thus giving rise to the universe's first dawn.

A related piece of atheological rhetoric suggests that searching for other worlds emphasis on the enormity of our cosmos attests to the tiny, and perhaps insignificant place we occupy in the cosmic scheme ... The quaint little stories of our conventional religious teachings seem but musings of children at play. 'However, it seems that our growing appreciation for the size of creation at least cuts both ways, for 'when one stares upward into a clear and dark night sky and out across the vast star fields of our galaxy, a sense of mystical astonishment is inevitable.

When one thinks of how small our galaxy is in the larger scheme of things, even greater wonder is inspired. This sense of cosmic wonder might motivate reflection upon the contingency, beauty and design of the heavens that has led many to conclude that there is a designer behind the cosmos.

'What could be more clear or obvious when we look up to the sky and contemplate the heavens, than that there is some divinity of superior intelligence?' So wrote Cicero, the Roman statesman, orator, lawyer and philosopher, who served as consul in the year 63 BC and the majority of humanity has echoed this insight.

This concept lies at the heart of our modern cosmology, in which the entire universe – space, time and matter – is thought to have been born from nothing in a Big Bang and expanding at an accelerated rate ever since. The initial singularity was a gravitational singularity of seemingly infinite density thought to have contained all the mass and space-time of the Universe before quantum fluctuations caused it to rapidly expand in the Big Bang and subsequent inflation, creating the present-day Universe.

All signs seem to suggest that the universe arose from a deeper nothing — involving the absence of space itself. Some argue that space and time was extremely unstable state from which the production of "something" is pretty much inevitable. The question why there is something rather than nothing is often answered with circular, recursive arguments. For example, ours might not be the only universe out there — we might instead live in a set of infinite or parallel universes. Or, that we live in an oscillatory universe - cyclic repetition interpretation of the Big Bang where the first cosmological event was the result of the collapse of a previous universe.

The British philosopher, Bertrand Russell once gave a public lecture on astronomy. He described how the earth orbits around the sun and how the sun, in turn, orbits around the centre of a vast collection of stars called our galaxy. At the end of the lecture, a little old lady at the back of the room got up and said: "What you have told us is rubbish. The world is really a flat plate supported on the back of a giant tortoise." The philosopher gave a superior smile, as the story goes, before replying, "What is the tortoise standing on?" "You're very clever, young man, very clever", said the old lady. "But it's turtles all the way down.

The secular version of the problem is "If the Big Bang caused everything, what caused the Big Bang?" The religious version is, "If God caused everything, what caused God?" It's always been odd to me that both atheists and theists use this exact same problem to point out that the "other side" is irrational. But there's an easy answer: "I don't know." "I don't know" is not an irrational stance. It's an intellectually honest one that anyone, regardless of his beliefs, can give.

Today we weave theories based on rigorous scientific investigation. Our ancestors wove cosmological theories based on imagination and belief. Like modern science, the creation myths found in all cultures all share a common feature: they describe the ordering of the cosmos from a state of chaos, and represent the earliest attempts to explain in symbolic narratives of the beginning of the world some of the most profound questions about the nature and origin of the universe.

Judaism, Christianity and Islam all share the same six-stage narrative of the creation that is expounded in Genesis 1. But, further back in human history and in all cultures, there have been stories that told of how the world was created from nothing.

Here's a remarkable example, from one of the oldest extant texts in any Indo-European language. The Rigveda is an ancient Indian collection of Vedic Sanskrit hymns. It is one of the four canonical sacred texts of Hinduism known as the Vedas. It was probably composed in the north-western region of the Indian subcontinent between 1500 and 1200 BC. It contains this: The Creation Hymn of Rig Veda.

There was neither non-existence nor existence then.
There was neither the realm of space nor the sky which
is beyond.
What stirred?
Where?

In whose protection?
Was there water, bottomless and deep?

There was neither death nor immortality then.
There was no distinguishing sign of night nor of day.
That One breathed, windless, by its own impulse.
Other than that there was nothing beyond.

Darkness was hidden by darkness in the beginning,
with no distinguishing sign, all this was water.
The life force that was covered with emptiness,
that One arose through the power of heat.

Desire came upon that One in the beginning,
that was the first seed of mind.
Poets seeking in their heart with wisdom
found the bond of existence and non-existence.
Their cord was extended across.
Was there below?
Was there above?
There were seed-placers, there were powers.
There was impulse beneath, there was giving forth
above.

Who really knows?
Who will here proclaim it?
Whence was it produced?
Whence is this creation?
The gods came afterwards, with the creation of this
universe.
Who then knows whence it has arisen?

Whence this creation has arisen
– perhaps it formed itself, or perhaps it did not –
the One who looks down on it,

in the highest heaven, only He knows
or perhaps He does not know.

It's important to note - it's not that these galaxies are moving away from us, it's the space and time between the galaxies that's expanding. Imagine you were travelling on a road made out of rubber at 5 MPH and it was 5 miles long. As you start travelling down the road you expect your trip to take 1 hour. However, the road is stretching 1 mile longer every 10 minutes. Thus your 5-mile road is now 11 miles long an hour later.

Who would have guessed that we're living in a universe that started from nothing and has been growing; actually, expanding at an accelerating rate ever since. Moreover, we can only travel at most at speed of light and the universe is expanding so if you set out today and travelled for 46 billion light years at near the speed of light the edge of the universe would be an additional 46 billion light years farther away plus whatever factor of expansion (which is believed to be speeding up.) There is neither end nor any centre because everything was once in the centre.

The known universe has a diameter of 93 billion light years. This includes the 13.8 billion light-years distance we can observe in all directions, (currently believed to be the age of the universe) plus the additional distance due to the expansion of the universe and expansion of empty space between any two distant points. Due to the expansion of the space if you had a magic ruler that reached instantly from here to the end of the universe in any direction it would be 46 - 47 billion light-years long instead of just 13.8 billion light years.

Is it any wonder that our search for extraterrestrials has been unsuccessful so far – Jill Tarter, the American astronomer best known for her work on the search for extraterrestrial intelligence said of searching for E.T, "It's like searching a glass of seawater for evidence of fish in all Earth's oceans." Space is so vast that the search for extraterrestrials so far have done little more than scratch the surface.

This new mathematical model suggests that signs of extraterrestrial intelligence could be common, for all we know — we've barely begun investigating the vastness where they might lie. The Fermi paradox is the contrast between the likelihood of life existing elsewhere in the universe and the lack of evidence for it. This is a significant conundrum. On the one hand, there is a strong sense that the conditions on Earth that led to the emergence of life cannot be unique.

This makes it seem likely that life must be common. But on the other, astronomers have scoured the cosmic haystack for the needle that would represent signs of intelligent life elsewhere in the universe and come up with nothing. As a result, many observers have concluded that there are no obvious signs.

The volume of three-dimensional space that can be searched is the volume of the universe centred on our solar system out to a specific distance. Wright and co define this as 10 kiloparsecs—about 30,000 light-years, or roughly the distance to the globular clusters that orbit the Milky Way galaxy. And, the statistical probability of us being the only life in our galaxy, let alone universe, are vanishingly small - basically to the point of impossibility. But yes, there is a but, of course, just because there is no good evidence that extraterrestrials are visiting us, that doesn't mean that we are alone in the universe.

The problem is, if anyone out there is alive, they are an awfully long way away. Space is huge! Here's an example: if you shrank the earth down to be one inch across, the sun would be about 985 feet away, and the nearest star would be about 50,000 miles away. And that's just the nearest star. There are billions of stars out there that are millions of times farther away.

Light can travel at the fastest known speed because it has no mass; it moves at 671,000,000 miles per hour. Ion propulsion engines, the best technologically feasible idea we now have can propel a spacecraft at 200,000 mph (in comparison, the Space Shuttles can reach speeds around 18,000 mph) and so reach the nearest star in something like 75,000 years. What might be the objective of extraterrestrials, their politics, their culture, their needs and beliefs to warrant the investment and expense, not to mention the serious logistical problems keeping anyone alive over the 75,000-year trip?

The idea of interstellar travel is, at least for now, awfully, incredibly, naïvely, amazingly, staggeringly optimistic. Carl Sagan, who was very interested in the search for extraterrestrials had this to say; "If it is just us [in the universe] it seems like an awful waste of space." But we are here, and it is for us to make the best of what we have, what we've been given.

As mentioned, whilst the Big Bang theory is currently the best theory we have, a number of issues remain unanswered. The beginning in particular, the infinitely dense description seems to be at odds with everything else in physics, and especially quantum mechanics and its uncertainty principle. Some speculate that ours might not be the only universe out there — we might instead live in a set of infinite or parallel universes, a multiverse.

Infinite universes are a consequence of several scientific theories; for instance, if spacetime truly goes on forever it might start repeating eventually, since particles can only be arranged a finite number of ways. A multiverse could also arise from "bubble universes," pockets of space in an inflating universe that are never able to meet; or parallel universes, where multiple 3-dimension universes are held in higher-dimensional space, unable to interact. While some universes in a multiverse might be like our own, others could have wildly different laws of physics and fundamental constants.

The idea of the multiverse comes about because in physics terms, our universe is very lucky to exist at all. What I didn't say earlier, when I was talking about how the Big Bang unfolded there is another important component to the universe that we hardly know at all – dark matter and dark energy.

Moreover, the amount of these components was, are, regarded crucial to us finding life here on Earth. We know how much dark energy there is because we know how it affects the universe's expansion. Other than that, it is a complete mystery. But it is an important mystery. It turns out that roughly 68% of the universe is dark energy. Dark matter makes up about 27%. The rest - everything on Earth, everything ever observed with all of our instruments, all normal matter - adds up to less than 5% of the universe. Come to think of it, maybe it shouldn't be called "normal" matter at all, since it is such a small fraction of the universe.

If dark energy were a lot stronger, the Universe would have been driven apart not only before the first stars and galaxies formed, but even before the first stable atoms could form. If it were stronger in the opposite (negative) direction, the Universe would have re-collapsed before anything interesting could have formed. The fact that dark energy is as weak as we observe it to be is one of the greatest cosmic coincidences of all, and one that's seemingly necessary for our existence.

Current theories predict there should be much more dark energy inside of our own universe than there is. That is a problem because adding more dark energy would lead it to expand so quickly that any matter would be diluted before it could form the stars or planets that we need to live. In response to that, some have suggested that we might in fact be living inside of a multiverse.

There are in fact lots of different universes – many of which will have more dark energy and so could not host life – and we simply live inside one that worked out in the right way. But new studies suggest that we might have been overstating how lucky we are. It might actually be possible for stars and planets to form even if there is much more dark energy. That is other parts of the multiverse would be far more hospitable to life than we had previously thought.

I make mention of the multiverse for two reasons – I figure if you have got this far in the book, you are clearly interested in the science, the physics of the universe as well as what I have to say about UFOs. Because the distance between stars makes interstellar travel impractical using conventional means some have sought to explain the UFO's as interdimensional visitation.

Simply put, UFOs are not spacecraft, but rather devices that travel between different realities and/or other dimensions that coexist separately but alongside our own. This has an unexpected advantage, well perhaps convenience, that proclaims UFOs to be the modern manifestation of a phenomenon that has occurred throughout recorded human history, which in prior ages were ascribed to mythological or supernatural creatures. I cover the idea of the multiverse in a little more detail in the next chapter.

This says nothing, however, as to why the "interdimensionals" resemble life on Earth. Engorged heads, long arms and legs, buggy eyes that find sense in remote, deserted location, country roads or woodland in the cover of night.

8. The meaning of reality

"The Lord God is subtle, but he is not malicious."

Einstein, a remark made during his first visit to Princeton

And later

"I have second thoughts. Maybe God is malicious after all."

University, Apr. 1921

According to Valentine Bargmann, one of Einstein's collaborators, what Einstein meant was that God makes us believe we understand something when in reality we are very far from it.

These remarks reflect Einstein's lifelong discomfort with the principles of the new science, quantum mechanics. Einstein wasn't necessarily provincial or vainglorious, he, as we shall see rejected decisive conclusions his own work foretold as well. This, even after they were pointed out to him.

Einstein's vacillations recall the words of Arthur Eddington, the British physicist and one of Einstein's most tireless champions: *"Not only is the universe stranger than we imagine, it is stranger than we can imagine."*

One of history's most expansive minds was, paradoxically, unable to accept the boundless oddities of Nature. It may well be due to the workings of quantum mechanics that we are alone in this universe.

After the mid 1920's the mainstream physics began to follow the course of the new quantum mechanics (and more recently String and Holographic Principles) a theory, which has often been described as breathtaking in its beauty and weird beyond that we can ever imagine. The implications of quantum mechanics render the reassuring world of our senses to be a tiny sliver of an infinitely weirder and more wonderful universe. More so than even we had ever conceived in our wildest fantasies.

Although quantum mechanics describes the behaviour of matter and energy at the sub-atomic scale, its utility has been vital in explaining aspects of stellar evolution, chemical reactions, and is responsible for the technological advances that make modern life possible. More fundamentally, it explains properties such as light, shape, colour, texture, hardness and the way almost everything interacts and fits together. It underpins and encompasses everything from the biochemistry of life to why we can't walk through solid walls.

However, as predictions go, this theory is largely probabilistic - that is, even in the presence of exacting knowledge, say of a falling raindrop, it is impossible to predict its future definitively regardless of how much care we take in such a prediction.

Einstein, arguably the most revolutionary thinker of modern times struggled greatly with quantum mechanics. He became the most prominent critic of the new theory believing the way ahead for fundamental physics was to develop the geometrical approach of his general relativity theory, as mentioned earlier, an amalgamated theory of space, time and gravitation, into an all-encompassing unified theory within which the results of the new quantum theory would be derived.

Some call this a "theory of everything", others more optimistically, "a final theory". And, Einstein as if seeking to further legitimatize his viewpoint more than once spoke for his God; I am convinced, he said, that "He does not play dice", and "whoever undertakes to set himself up as a judge of truth and knowledge is shipwrecked by the laughter of the Gods."

According to one author Einstein was searching for a theory that not only reconciled general relativity to quantum mechanics, but it reconciled Science and the Bible as well - an undertaking by anyone's reckoning.

The new science doesn't just demand us to rethink lofty concerns such as the shape and size of the universe, space and time, or of the role subatomic particles may play in co-creating multi-worlds and multi-histories, or even whether a Prime Mover (God) is needed at all, but also how the consciousness of human agents enters into the structure of physical phenomena.

The principles of quantum mechanics contradict the older idea that local mechanical processes alone can account for the structure of all observed phenomena. The new science brings directly and irreducibly into the overall causal structure certain psychologically described choices made by human agents about how they will act.

Our experience tells us that our reality is made up of physical material, and that our world is an independently existing objective one. However, according to the new science reality is far beyond human perception and most certainly intuition. We have difficulty explaining consciousness in terms of material as chemical and physical processes.

How for example can the interaction of physical objects give rise to something as immaterial as experience, emotion, or feeling? It is conceivable that consciousness and reality are not as separate as material science would have us believe. And from this comes a shocking truth that may force us to rethink the nature of reality itself.

Quantum mechanics teaches us that the way subatomic particles such as Quarks, Gluons, and Photons behave and interact is fundamental to the way the universe works. Indeed, the "Standard Model" of particle physics, the theory that describes the behaviour of subatomic particles is currently the most accepted theory of the universe.

For this reason, it is sometimes regarded as a "theory of almost everything". And, perhaps because of their privileged preeminent status, subatomic particles need not submit to our everyday sensibilities. Amit Gozwami in his 1993 book, "The Self-Aware Universe" sketches out some of their more enigmatic peculiarities.

Subatomic particles can be at more than one location at the same time. They cease to exist here and simultaneously appear over there without traveling the intervening space. Pressing one subatomic particle by a conscious mind simultaneously influences its correlated twin particle, no matter how far apart they are. Subatomic particles are not located in ordinary space and time until they are being watched.

Einstein spent the second part of his life trying to develop an all-encompassing theory that would at last unify his theory of general relativity with quantum mechanics, reconciling the large-scale structures of the universe with the very small. And, although this work would engender intense scepticism there was much reason for Einstein's doggedness and resolve. After all, general relativity is regarded a basic theory for all of physics, and one of the greatest intellectual achievements of the 20th century. As far as human achievement goes, it is up there with King Lear or Dvořák's New World No 9. It is also one of the most audacious ideas of modern science, quite literally giving the universe order, shape and structure.

Einstein's notion of space-time isn't an easy concept to grasp at first. It is counter to our intuition; we can't, for example, see it when we look up at the skies. As discussed in the previous chapter we can't feel it when we drive around town. The theory relies on a great deal of advanced mathematical structures and techniques. In fact, until very recently, general relativity was taught only in postgraduate mathematics or physics courses, because the mathematical foundations of the theory were regarded as much too demanding for undergraduate students.

Nevertheless, it is handy to try and get some sense of this breakthrough, if for no other reason than to shock our senses into tolerating strangeness that lies just beyond our everyday experiences. The significance of this theory can be appreciated when we survey prevailing tenets vis-à-vis gravity at the beginning of the 20th century; the tenets Einstein, at the tender age of 26 miraculously overturned. To do this we must first go back some 350 years; to a time when Great Britain and greater Europe were gradually emerging out of the Middle-ages; men, God-fearing and unworthy by virtue and stained by original sin now, with greater hast entering the so-called age of reason, the Renaissance.

Changes in philosophy and science ensued quickly and natural philosophers such as the Newton, Galilei and Harvey began to be understood as scientist. The intrusion of newly invented machines became part of the daily and economic lives and the science of chemistry developed from medieval alchemy, and the 17th century science of astronomy evolved from astrology.

Profound religious beliefs gave way to scientific reasoning and staple creationism began, slowly at first, to revel itself as inherently mechanical and predictable - prompting Newton to call God "the Divine Watchmaker". This of course didn't happen without resistance. Theological arguments, particularly those based in confessionalism, opposed accepting change and continued to exert a powerful influence on the vision of the world and the interpretation of Nature, even if the two worlds, that of faith and that of science, were slowly separating.

During this period of ideological change Newton formulated his famous law of universal gravitation – arising it is said from an astonishing piece of insight. He compared the acceleration of the Moon to the acceleration of objects here on Earth. Just how much did the apple tree inspire Newton has been much debated. William Stukeley, in his Memoirs of Newton's Life recalls a 1726 conversation with Newton. *"We went into the garden and drank tea under the shade of some apple trees, only he, and myself. Amidst other discourse, he told me, he was just in the same situation, as when formerly, and the notion of gravitation came into his mind. Why should that apple always descend perpendicularly to the ground?"*

Believing that gravitational forces were responsible for each. For the first time a physical law, moreover a product of man, seemed to completely describe the influence of gravity here on Earth and elsewhere.

And, whilst Newton acknowledged a monotheistic God as the masterful creator whose existence could not be denied, he apparently didn't see contradictions between religion and his science. They simply further maintained that while the natural world operates without the direct intervention of God, his existence, along with that of human beings, is part of a larger teleological plan that reflects his intent.

According to Newton every object with mass exerts an attractive force on every other object. The magnitude of the force is inversely proportional to the square of the distance. Although Newton never provided an explanation for gravity, he most certainly gave us a means to make sense of and calculate the motion of things [affected] by gravity – all things; cannonballs, footballs and as mentioned celestial bodies too. In fact, Newton's work has served us well – its utility has enabled the launch of countless satellites, track icy comets, and even fly man to the Moon.

And about the same time in Germany scientific psychology began as a physiological psychology born of a marriage between the philosophy of mind, and the experimental phenomenology that arose within sensory physiology. Philosophical psychology, concerned with the epistemological problem of the nature of knowing the mind in relationship to the world as known, contributed fundamental questions and explanatory constructs; sensory physiology and to a certain extent physics contributed experimental methods and a growing body of phenomenological facts.

In 1690 John Locke distinguished between primary and secondary qualities. Primary qualities, he believed, such as solidity are completely inseparable from the bodies in which they inhabit. These, according to Locke are perceived by our senses. Secondary qualities are powers inherent in objects to produce sensations in the perceiver such as colour, odour, or sound. Interestingly, these qualities did not themselves exist in objects. Locke and others tried to ambush problems of perceptual illusion by distinguishing between the material objects and the ideas by means of which we perceive them.

George Berkeley, the Bishop of Cloyne on the other hand proffered that this representationalist approach can provide no reliable account of the connection between the qualities (ideas) and the objects they are supposed to represent. A God was still involved in Berkeley's immaterialistic philosophy. Locke's notion of secondary qualities was now expanded to include primary qualities and taken out of objects and placed in both God and, for the first time the mind.

So as far back as the late 1600's, the so-called defender of common sense, Berkeley held that what we perceive really is as we perceive it to be. However, the things we perceive are just sensible objects, collections of sensible qualities, which are themselves nothing other than ideas that exist within our minds.

Something that quantum mechanics re-invokes, albeit minus the role of God. For instance, Fritjof Capra, the author of The Tao of Physics (1975) and The Hidden Connections (2002) writes: "The crucial feature of atomic physics is that the human observer is not only necessary to observe the properties of an object but is necessary even to define these properties.

Whilst the implications and implementations of quantum mechanics are many, there are wool-headed individuals who have taken the weirder consequences of Quantum Mechanics and used it to claim some sort of scientific basis to some kind of mysticism. Quantum mechanics has been presented in the form of an Intelligent Design argument processed through the most stereotyped of post-modernist "reality is a social construction" deconstructionism.

For many philosophers of this period the universe, at the very deepest level, contained only two categories of entity: substances and modes. Modes are synonymous to Locke's secondary qualities. But ultimately all modes exist in something which is not itself a mode, that is, in a substance.

Given the foundational role substance played in the metaphysical schemes of most thinkers of the time it is not surprising to find that theories of substance underlie dramatically different accounts of the nature and structure of reality. The existence of God on the other hand was not only a given but God's existence was absolutely independent of all substance – the ultimate independent being, God the substance par excellence. And this wasn't necessarily just a 17th century conception. In the second half of the 4th century BC the treatise by Aristotle talk of only three kinds of substances; God, heavenly spheres, and animals and plants.

Despite the momentous accomplishments Newton achieved. Einstein realized that Newtonian gravity was just an illusion and that it is space itself that is distorted. General relativity proposes that space and time dimensions are interchangeable and massive objects cause a distortion in space-time. Imagine setting a large body in the centre of a trampoline. The body would press down into the fabric, causing it to dimple. A marble rolled around the edge would spiral inward toward the body, pulled in much the same way that the gravity of a planet pulls at rocks in space.

As mentioned in the previous chapter, when Einstein published his theory, it was assumed that the universe was made up of stars whose distribution was relatively uniform throughout space. Also, as mentioned the overall size of the universe was unchanging. Einstein himself knew that having a uniform distribution of matter would be problematic.

He reasoned, if space-time is going to curve due to the presence of matter then those regions of space-time with more matter are going to preferentially attract more and more matter, thus forming regions of intense gravitational fields or black holes! Einstein dismissed the existence of holes in space, perhaps foretelling what a mess the math would be.

Einstein once described himself as a "deeply religious nonbeliever." By such a statement he meant that his worldview was somehow pervaded by an overwhelming and general feeling of religiosity rather than dominated by some specific creedal commitment.

Perhaps Einstein's curiosity in the Eucharist might be easier to fathom were we to regard it as a symptom of his abiding and lifelong quest to unravel the eternal enigma of appearance and reality. Relativity theory, in its special and general forms, and, even more iconoclastically, quantum mechanics as we shall see, together caused a complete revolution in human understanding of the physical world, the consequences of which are still to be absorbed into philosophy – and hardly yet into theology.

An important matter is the future of the universe. Does the universe have an eschatological purpose? Or what kind of future is there? Big Bang cosmology opened the window within science toward transcendent creation in the past while apparently closing the window to redemptive eschatology for the distant future. Observations suggest that the expansion of the universe will continue forever. If so, the universe will cool as it expands, eventually becoming too cold to sustain life, any life. For this reason, this future scenario is popularly called the Big Freeze.

When living in truly interesting times, we expect the truly unexpected. Many now think that this idea should not be limited to just black holes. Some think that information about all things; is spread across the far edge of the universe. The universe therefore is nothing more than a projection of a holographic film. Whether we actually live in a hologram is, with good reason, being hotly debated. Having said this, it is now becoming more and more clear that looking at physical phenomena through a holographic lens could be key to solving the greatest riddle of all – us!

I am reminded of Corinthians 15:51 - Behold, I tell you a mystery; we will not all sleep, but we will all be changed.

A key feature of quantum theory is the prediction that sub-particles can exist in a superposition of states at the same time and only collapse down to a single state upon interaction with other particles or observation by the external world. Many have linked the collapse of the wave function by the sentient conscious. That is, it takes a sentient being to "make" reality.

"If a tree falls in a forest and no one is around to hear it, does it make a sound" philosophical thought experiment that raises question regarding observation and perception that goes back to the 18th century.

Einstein is reported to have asked his fellow physicist and friend Niels Bohr, one of the founding fathers of quantum mechanics, whether he realistically believed that "the moon does not exist if nobody is looking at it." To this Bohr replied that however hard he (Einstein) may try, he would not be able to prove that it does, thus giving the entire riddle the status of a kind of infallible conjecture — one that cannot be either proved or disproved.

Quantum mechanics, however, does seem to defy the common-sense notions of causality, locality and realism. For example, you know that the moon exists even when you're not looking at it, that's realism. Causality tells us that if you flick a light switch, the bulb will illuminate. And thanks to a hard limit on the speed of light, if you flick a switch now, the related effect could not occur instantly a million light-years away according to locality.

However, these principles break down in the quantum realm. Perhaps the most famous example is quantum entanglement, which says that particles on opposite sides of the universe can be intrinsically linked so that they share information instantly—an idea that made Einstein called "spooky."

It should be said that macroscopic consequences of Quantum Mechanics are numerous, valuable, and something potentially very cool. For example, the entire computer industry is built on quantum mechanics. Modern semiconductor-based electronics rely on the band structure of solid objects. This is fundamentally a quantum phenomenon, depending on the wave nature of electrons, and because we understand that wave nature, we can manipulate the electrical properties of silicon.

As insinuated, many scientists at the time that quantum theory was being developed in the 1920's and 1930's drifted from science into the realm of philosophy and stated that quantum particles only collapse to a single state when viewed by a conscious observer. I must admit, some of the proposals put out there in the name of quantum theory could perhaps belongs in science fiction.

Erwin Schrödinger, the Austrian Nobel Laureate physicist found this concept absurd and devised his thought experiment to make plain the absurd yet logical outcome of such claims.

In Schrodinger's imaginary experiment, you place a cat in a box with a tiny bit of radioactive substance. When the radioactive substance decays, it triggers a Geiger counter which causes a poison or explosion to be released that kills the cat. Now, the decay of the radioactive substance is governed by the laws of quantum mechanics. This means that the atom starts in a combined state of "going to decay" and "not going to decay".

If we apply the observer-driven idea to this case, there is no conscious observer present (everything is in a sealed box), so the whole system stays as a combination of the two possibilities. The cat ends up both dead and alive at the same time. Because the existence of a cat that is both dead and alive at the same time is absurd and does not happen in the real world, this thought experiment shows that wavefunction collapse is not just driven by conscious observers.

The decoherence approaches to interpreting quantum theory have been further explored and developed, including one that implies that all possible alternate histories and futures are real, each representing an actual "world" or "universe." In layman's terms, the hypothesis states there is a very large, perhaps infinite, number of universes, and everything that could possibly have happened in our past, but did not, has occurred in the past of some other universe or universes.

From this comes the notion that a Many Worlds, or parallel universes quantum model might provide one of the only possible explanations for our existence. Picture an elementary particle, like an electron. If you think of all the things that an electron could do in the next fraction of a second, you'd have quite a long list: it might move to the left, move to the right, move up, move down, jiggle a bit, spin clockwise, etc, etc.

I should say before going much further, there are 3 different types of subatomic particles that together make an atom. These are Protons, Neutrons, and electrons. The centre of the atom is called the nucleus. Also, the atom is mostly empty space. For example, a Hydrogen atom is about 99.99999999% empty space. Put another way, if a hydrogen atom were the size of the Earth, the Proton at its centre would be about 200 meters (600 feet) across.

Protons and Neutrons are in turn made up of elementary particles. The Electron is itself an elementary particle. The 12 elementary particles of matter are six quarks (up, charm, top, Down, Strange, Bottom) 3 electrons (electron, muon, tau) and three neutrinos (e, muon, tau). Four of these elementary particles would suffice in principle to build the world around us: the up and down quarks, the electron and the electron neutrino.

And whilst I'm here, let me say, in the world of particle physics, the term particle zoo is used colloquially to describe a relatively extensive list of the then known "elementary particles" by comparison to the variety of species in a zoo (see Fig two below.)

Fig Two. From matter molecules to strings

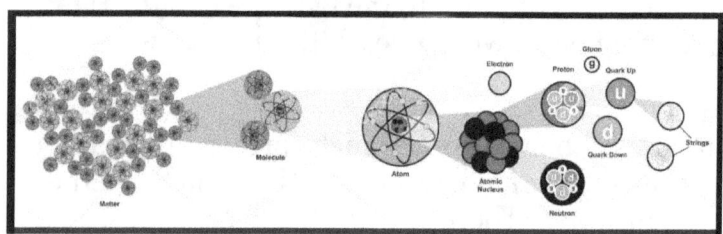

In the history of particle physics, the situation was particularly confusing in the late 1960s. Before the discovery of quarks, hundreds of strongly interacting particles (hadrons) were known and believed to be distinct elementary particles in their own right. It was later discovered that they were not elementary particles, but rather composites of the quarks. The set of particles believed today to be elementary is known as the Standard Model and includes quarks, bosons and leptons.

And then there are strings. In physics, string theory is a theoretical frame-work in which the point-like particles such as quarks are composed of one-dimensional objects called strings. It's one of the most brilliant, controversial and unproven ideas in all of physics. At the heart of string theory is the thread of an idea that's run through physics for centuries, that at some fundamental level, all the different forces, particles, interactions and manifestations of reality are tied together as part of the same framework.

Quantum mechanics tells us that the atom, actually, the elementary particle never actually chooses to go with any one of those options, and instead does them all at the same time, a kind of a Schizophrenic existence. And since that's happening to every atom and subatomic particle in the universe, the end result is that essentially, anything that can happen does happen, in a different branch of the multiverse.

The way quantum field theory works is that you take a particle and you perform a mathematical "sum over histories." You can't just calculate where the particle was and where it is and how it got to be there, since there's an inherent, fundamental quantum uncertainty to nature. Instead, you add up all the possible ways it could have arrived at its present state, appropriately weighted probabilistically, and that's how you calculate the state of a single particle.

So, as the theory goes, the multiverse ends up exploring every combination of particle positions and orientations that's physically possible, each combination of which gives rise to a different universe. And since one of those combinations leads to the evolution of the human species, well: here we are, in that particular branch of the multiverse (see Fig two below.) So as long as it's at least possible for life to evolve, it will evolve in some branch of the multiverse. Even if the odds are very, very low. It just happens that we are in just one of the many worlds.

Figure Three.

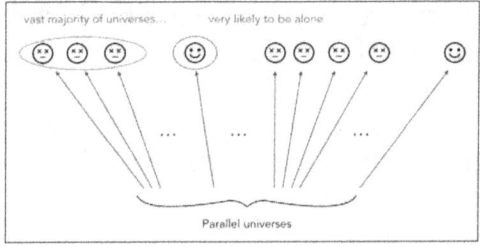

We often apply this question to life on Earth with the Goldilocks principle, which ponders why Earth is "just right" for life. The anthropic principle tackles an even greater question: Why is the universe itself just right for life?

For instance, when we compare the electromagnetic force to gravity, we find that electromagnetism is 39 times stronger. And that's handy because if the two powers were more evenly matched, stars wouldn't burn long enough for life to develop on an orbiting planet, an anthropic coincidence, or a coincidence related to mankind's very existence.

Another example involves the vacuum - a vacuum in the universe is a lot less dense than we previously thought (139 times less dense, in fact). That's significant because if the original higher estimates had been correct, the universe would have blown apart eons ago.

That's the anthropic principle in a nutshell: if the multiverse is real, there really isn't anything strange about the fact that we find ourselves in exactly the kind of universe that would allow for our own existence. In fact, we couldn't help but for that to be the case.

If life is phenomenally unlikely, there are going to be more branches of the multiverse without life than with life. But what about the rare universes that actually do contain life?

Well, just like you wouldn't expect a lottery winner to win twice, the odds against life evolving a second time in the same universe would be incredibly low. It would happen in some universes, of course, but in the vast majority of "life" universes, you'd expect that life to be alone.

Without the multiverse, it would take a major conspiracy of nature to explain how we might possibly be alone in the universe. The cosmic coin would have to be insanely biased. The multiverse allows us to account for our existence even if the odds of life evolving are as close to zero as makes a difference — and it may be one of the only ways of doing so.

9. Life from nothing

How did life begin? There can hardly be a bigger question. For much of human history, almost everyone believed some version involving Gods hand. Any other explanation was inconceivable.

Charles Darwin, a man with an Anglican school education, whose aim of becoming a clergyman went to the University of Cambridge for the required Bachelor of Arts degree, which included studies of Anglican theology, someone bearing knowledge in Genesis and the Bible.

He took great interest in natural history and became filled with zeal for science as defined by John Herschel, based on the natural theology of William Paley which presented the argument from divine design in nature to explain adaptation as God acting through laws of nature.

And, on the voyage of the Beagle he remained orthodox and looked for "centres of creation" to explain distribution, but towards the end of the voyage he began to doubt that species were fixed. By this time, he was critical of the Bible as history, and wondered why all religions should not be equally valid. Following his return in October 1836, he developed his novel ideas of geology while speculating about transmutation of species and thinking about religion.

In the introduction of his 1871 book, The Descent of Man, he would write *"Ignorance more frequently begets confidence than does knowledge: it is those who know little, and not those who know much, who so positively assert that this or that problem will never be solved by science."*

The genius of Darwin in "The Origin of Species" (1859) was that he brought together previously unrelated aspects to biology; Variation and selection (leading to Natural Selection), the Geological Record, Geographical Distribution and the "Mutual Affinities of Organic Beings".

Creationist claim that Darwin himself realized that it seemed incredible that evolutionary processes had to explain the human eye. The quote is often used by them in an effort to convince their credulous followers that Darwin had doubts about some aspects of evolution. The problem is that they often only use the first few lines and omit the part beginning "Yet reason tells me,...".

One of the main "gaps" in Darwin's theory was the problem of inheritance or genetics. The solution to this was provided by Gregor Mendel in the 1860s but remained unknown until the turn of the century.

Darwinian biology tells a whole new story of creation, one that cannot be literally reconciled with religious creation stories such as those narrated in the book of Genesis. A quote from Genesis 1:26 then God said,

> "*Let Us make man in Our image, according to Our likeness; and let them rule over the fish of the sea and over the birds of the sky and over the cattle and over all the earth, and over every creeping thing that creeps on the earth.*"

Could Genesis be telling such a story? Is it possible to see the connection between this story of creation that was not observed by any human witnesses but still accepted as a part of our rich faith tradition that claims God as the Creator and any attempt to tell this story pales in comparison to the act of creation itself?

As creations of God, imaged to mirror the divine image, we live somewhere between the anonymity of a sea of nameless faces in a universe that cannot be measured and yet with the realization that God knows each one of us in minute detail. The problem with holding to a literal interpretation is that there's not just one story of creation to describe what God did; there are two. Not surprising to the ever-whimsical nature of God, the Bible doesn't flinch about laying them alongside one another, even with all their differences.

The first story is an experience of hearing God speak the world into being. God's words shoot off into the darkness and the nothingness and the nothing becomes something. The second story isn't auditory; there are no verbal commands making the world. Instead, the story is more like a drama. God is less a preacher and more a sculptor, bending down to scoop up a lump of clay to shape a new being into creation, through a process.

But central to the current cultural debates over evolution versus creation is the question of how God actually creates. Many modern Christians argue that the Bible teaches that God created plants, animals and especially humans through direct "special creation" without mediating such creation through any so-called natural causes. "Special creationist" Christians hold that the idea of God's "indirectly" creating through "natural processes" is a concept entirely foreign to the witness of Scripture.

According to these believers, Scripture unambiguously confesses that human beings, both as a species and as individuals are in particular created by exemplary supernatural events that are distinctive from the processes whereby God creates the rest of the natural world. Many have shown, elsewhere, however, the context and usage of various Hebrew terms describing God's creative activity affirm an understanding of God's creating plants, animals, and even humans through non-instantaneous processes. That is, the distinction between direct special creation and indirect creation through natural law is a false and unscriptural dichotomy is false.

But how about another process of kind - the story of life's birth on Earth. Over the last century, a few scientists have tried to figure out how the first life might have sprung up. They have even tried to recreate this Genesis moment in their labs: to create brand-new life from scratch. So far nobody has managed it, but we have come a long way. Advances in fields as disparate as astronomy, planetary science and chemistry now hold promise that answers to such profound questions may be around the corner.

Life is old. The dinosaurs are perhaps the most famous extinct creatures, and they had their beginnings 250 million years ago. But life dates back much further. The oldest known fossils are around 3.5 billion years old, 14 times the age of the oldest dinosaurs. But the fossil record may stretch back still further.

For instance, in August 2016 researchers found what appear to be fossilised microbes dating back 3.7 billion years. According to radiometric dating and other sources of evidence, Earth formed over 4.5 billion years ago from the swirling dust and gas remnants of an old star's supernova explosion. As the molten mass settled and cooled, a solid crust soon formed, probably within as little as about 150 million years, along with a rudimentary atmosphere composed largely of carbon dioxide, water vapor and nitrogen. So, if life was formed on Earth, it was born in the billion years between Earth coming into existence and the preservation of the oldest known fossils.

Although the environment at that time would have been highly hazardous to life, the necessary ingredients were all present in some form; liquid water, the chemical building blocks (usually taken to be the six elements: oxygen, hydrogen, carbon, nitrogen, sulphur and phosphorus) and some kind of energy source such as ultraviolet light from the Sun, electrical energy from lightning or chemical energy from deep-sea, and hydrothermal vents, all of which would have been available on the early Earth.

Energy from thermal vents, as we shall see, will prove crucial in creating a gradient in positively charged protons that served as a "battery" to fuel the creation of organic molecules and proto-cells.

In the 1920s, Russian scientist Aleksandr Oparin and English scientist J. B. S. Haldane both separately proposed what's now called the Oparin-Haldane hypothesis: that life on Earth could have arisen step-by-step from non-living matter through a process of "gradual chemical evolution."

Oparin and Haldane thought that the early Earth had a reducing atmosphere, meaning an oxygen-poor atmosphere in which molecules tend to donate electrons. Under these conditions, they suggested that simple inorganic molecules could have been fuelled with energy from lightning or the sun to form building blocks like amino acids and nucleotides, which could have accumulated in the oceans, making a "primordial soup." The building blocks could have combined in further reactions, forming larger, more complex molecules (polymers) like proteins and nucleic acids, perhaps in pools at the water's edge.

The polymers could have assembled into units or structures that were capable of sustaining and replicating themselves. Oparin thought these might have been "colonies" of proteins clustered together to carry out metabolism, while Haldane suggested that macromolecules became enclosed in membranes to make cell-like structures.

Whilst the specific details of this model are probably not quite correct. For instance, geologists now think the early atmosphere was not reducing, and it's unclear whether pools at the edge of the ocean are a likely site for life's first appearance. But the basic idea – a stepwise, spontaneous formation of simple, then more complex, then self-sustaining biological molecules or assemblies – is still at the core of most origins-of-life hypotheses today.

In the 1950s the iconic Miller-Urey experiment, which zapped a mixture of water and simple chemicals with electric pulses (to simulate the impact of lightning), demonstrated that amino acids, the building blocks of proteins, are easy to make.

Even though the atmosphere of early Earth was different than in Miller and Urey's setup (that is, not reducing, and not rich in ammonia and methane) a variety of experiments carried out in the years since have shown that organic building blocks, especially amino acids can form from inorganic precursors under a fairly wide range of conditions. From these experiments, it seems reasonable to imagine that at least some of life's building blocks could have formed abiotically on early Earth.

Monomers, molecule that can be bonded to other identical molecules to form a polymer may have been able to spontaneously form polymers under the conditions found on early Earth. For instance, in the 1950s, biochemist Sidney Fox and his colleagues found that if amino acids were heated in the absence of water, they could link together to form proteins. Fox suggested that, on early Earth, ocean water carrying amino acids could have splashed onto a hot surface like a lava flow, boiling away the water and leaving behind a protein.

Additional experiments in the 1990s showed that RNA nucleotides can be linked together when they are exposed to a clay surface clay acts as a catalyst to form an RNA polymer. More broadly, clay and other mineral surfaces may have played a key role in the formation of polymers, acting as supports or catalysts. Polymers floating in solution might have broken down quickly, supporting a surface-attached model.

Specific pathways that describe chemistry to life are not completely established, and consensus is not reached. The central reason hinges on the versatility of RNA, a very long molecule that plays a multitude of essential roles in all existing forms of life. RNA can not only act like an enzyme, it can also store and transmit information. Remarkably, all the protein in all organisms is made by the catalytic activity of the RNA component of the ribosome, the cellular machine that reads genetic information and makes protein molecules. This observation suggests that RNA dominated an early stage in the evolution of life.

There also many who contend the possibility of life from non-living origins – often arguing that if the naturalistic molecules-to-human-life evolution were true, multi-billions of links are required to bridge modern humans with the chemicals that once existed in the hypothetical "primitive soup."

The major links in the molecules-to-man theory that must be bridged include (a) evolution of simple molecules into complex molecules, (b) evolution of complex molecules into simple organic molecules, (c) evolution of simple organic molecules into complex organic molecules, (d) eventual evolution of complex organic molecules into DNA or similar information storage molecules, and (e) eventually evolution into the first cells. This process requires multimillions of links, all which either are missing or controversial. Scientists even lack plausible just-so stories for most of evolution. Furthermore, the parts required to provide life clearly have specifications that rule out most substitutions.

A lot can happen in 4.5 Billion years. Given all the events and circumstances that have transpired over this time — including the evolutionary twists and turns that occurred as the result of seemingly random processes — it's safe to say that the exact way life unfolded on Earth is cosmologically unique. But what about life, complex life, or technologically advanced life elsewhere?

If a planet was formed similar to Earth in the distant past, there are three big steps that must have occurred in order to get a recognizably advanced civilization like our own.

A. Life must have somehow arisen from non-life. It occurred at least once on Earth, more than 4 billion years ago. Has it occurred elsewhere in our Solar System and beyond?

B. Life must have thrived and evolved to become multicellular, complex, and differentiated. For billions of years, life on Earth was single-celled and relatively simple, with copying errors from one generation to the next providing the overwhelming amount of variation in organisms.

C. Intelligent life must have evolved, with the right traits to also become a technologically advanced civilization. This may be the step with the greatest uncertainty of all.

10. Extraterrestrials aren't comin' no more

Since around 2014 the number of UFO sightings have dropped dramatically. As well, many UFO interest groups have folded, in spite, of or perhaps partly because of the disclosure of numerous previously classified government documents. The decline in UFO sightings may be revealing that interest them is becoming a blip on the human cultural radar, a point in time thing – quant in the judgement of future generations in the same way a pedestrian waving a red flag or carrying a lantern used to warn bystanders of the approaching vehicles when self-propelled cars first appeared on London streets.

I'm convinced the UFO lore is a reflection of human culture, tied to the space age, motivated by conquering new existential frontiers. As suggested earlier, certainly, there is less credulity among the public for tales of the extraordinary. The standard explanation attributes this to growing scepticism.

It might not be a coincidence that the term UFO and some of the phenomena that surrounds it, abductions, and impossible technologies, are relatively recent. Before the 1940's, reports of sightings of objects in the sky were extremely rare. Centuries of recorded history give no clear indication of any such activity. Then, at the predawn of the space-age, around the time of the Roswell conspiracy, the UFO culture was born, giving rise to everything from Space Invaders to The X-Files and more.

After all, from the 1940s extraterrestrials were originally characterised as saviours who could help humans transcend the cold-war paranoia of nuclear annihilation; especially marked at the time, after two world wars.

The foundations laid by the invasion movies of the 1950s were also integral in creating mass hysteria and paranoia amongst movie-goers. Reflecting public fears and political themes, filmmakers explored the threat of nuclear warfare and infiltration of the Soviet Union through an alien invasion.

Events like Watergate and the Vietnam war fuelled distrust in government, UFOs came to be viewed more as a possible threat, and some came to believe their existence was verified or could be verified in secret military vaults.

As already stated, a great deal of UFO researchers would tell you that 98 per cent of UFO sightings are easily explainable. There are a great variety of natural phenomena, unusual and the less than remarkable. Man-made flying machines that are genuinely taken for all-together a different thing. In fact, with the recent take-up of drones all over the world I'm a little surprised that UFO sightings haven't instead been on the increase. The U.S Consumer Association, reported more than 2.4 million drones were sold in the US alone in 2016, more than double the figure for 2015.

Dozens of groups interested in the flying saucers and other unidentified craft have already shut-up shop. There is simply not the interest as in previous years yonder. High on the agenda for those groups that are still meeting is the question of whether the subject continues to have a future, have relevance.

At the time of writing this book, the Association for the Scientific Study of Anomalous Phenomena, a UK-based education and research charity, dedicated to the scientific investigation of alleged paranormal and anomalous phenomena, will be meeting to address the crisis in the subject and assess whether UFOs were a thing of the past.

According to data from US-based National UFO Reporting Centre the slump started in 2014, after years of sightings on the rise. Since the 1990's, the overall number of UFO observations steadily increased, reaching a peak of approximately 9,000 reports in 2014. After that, it all went quickly downhill.

The upcoming apocalypse as the end of the Mayan calendar approached in 2012, UFO sightings peaked - possibly due to certain sections of the public who were anticipating some form of an extraterrestrial

Armageddon. It should be stated, also, that UFO sightings reached their spate roughly within a decade of the release of Steven Spielberg's film Close Encounters of the Third Kind, the story of Roy Neary, an everyday blue-collar worker in Indiana, whose life changes after an encounter with an unidentified flying object.

Spielberg and Columbia Pictures had originally reached out to the US Air Force and NASA to provide their expertise, but both declined. It was rumoured that NASA strongly advised Spielberg not to produce Close Encounters at all. In a 1978 interview with Cinema Papers, Spielberg stated:

> "I really found my faith when I heard that the government was opposed to the film. If NASA took the time to write me a 20-page letter, then I knew there must be something happening."

The combination of nuclear warfare, infiltration of the Soviet Union, secret projects and films heightened suspicions that the US government knew something that millions of citizens were unaware of. During the 1970s, numerous researchers within the UFO community began to compile witness accounts of encounters and abductions with extra-terrestrial beings.

One good reason to believe there were never any UFOS is that nobody sees them anymore. Once, the skies were refulgent with extraterrestrial craft; now they are back to their primordial emptiness, returning only static to the radio telescopes, and offering the occasional meteor shower to the wondering eye.

If, for example they look at things on the balance of probabilities and this area of study has been ongoing for many decades, the lack of compelling evidence beyond the pure anecdotal suggests that on the balance of probabilities – there is nothing out there.

The Association for the Scientific Study of Anomalous Phenomena report that UFO cases have dropped by 96 per cent since 1988, while the number of groups involved in UFO research has fallen from well over 100 in the 1990s to around 30 now. Among those to have closed are the British Flying Saucer Bureau, the Northern UFO Network, and the Northern Anomalies Research Organisation.

At the same time, sightings that supposed UFO encounters took place surrounded by conspiracy theories have also dimensioned. The 1947 Roswell incident or UK's Rendlesham are amongst numerous examples of previously classified government files that have since been declassified. The Roswell incident led to one of the greatest extraterrestrial conspiracy theories, but the U.S. Air Force denied an extraterrestrial connection. As discussed, in the 1990s, the US Air Force said the object was actually a balloon that was searching for Soviet Union nuclear test signals under Project Mogul.

However, the incident did prompt official U.S. investigations into unidentified flying objects in the next few years. A report published for the U.S. Air Force's Project Sign stated that the things people saw were "real" but that at least "some of the incidents may be caused by natural phenomena" and others may be related to domestic or foreign aircraft. The Air Force's Project Grudge, which issued a report in 1949 prior to its shutdown in 1951, continued the investigation but found no conclusive evidence of UFOs.

Project Blue Book was yet another program from the U.S. Air Force, following up on Projects Sign and Grudge. The program conducted a series of studies between 1952 and 1969 to figure out if UFOs could hurt national security and to search for UFO data. More than 10,000 of those case files are now freely available on the Internet Archive.

According to Sapace.com, the Condon Committee, more formally known as the University of Colorado UFO Project, was a group funded by the Air Force that looked at UFOs under the leadership of physicist Edward Condon. The group re-examined the information from Project Blue Book and published its efforts in the "Scientific Study of Unidentified Flying Objects" in 1968.

The Condon Report found that about one-third of the cases couldn't be explained, even though the introduction stated that "further extensive study of

UFOs probably cannot be justified on the expectation that science will be advanced thereby." Some reports say that the ultimate purpose of the report was to stop U.S. investigations into UFOs. Whether or not that was true, Blue Book ceased operations in 1969, the year after the Condon Report was released.

And, even the CIA released previously classified documents in 2016 pertaining to strange UFO encounters, and there is an entire web page devoted to the agency's investigations between 1949 and 1990. The National Security Agency and the Federal Bureau of Investigation released further government documents.

The MuckRock website publishes regularly on U.S. government documents released under the Freedom of Information Act. As well as U.S documents, the website includes documents from Australia, Brazil, Britain, Canada, Denmark, France, New Zealand, Panama and Spain.

Belief in UFOs is definitely in a state of decline, along with much else that could be classed as paranormal. Part of the reason is that the technology for providing documentary evidence of such matters is now widely available to everybody with a smartphone, and such purported evidence as there is on YouTube looks extremely frayed.

It isn't so much that belief can exist without proof; it's that it must emphatically avoid proof to remain belief. We are in the process, paradoxically, of proving a negative hypothesis with UFOs: there never was any such thing.

Indeed, indisputable evidence of intelligent life coming to Earth could be the greatest news of all time. Yet, after thousands of anecdotal, photo, and video reports have accrued over decades, what are we to conclude? With the greatest balance of scepticism and "wanting to believe", all that can confidently be asserted is that some objects, appearing in the sky on film or video, seem unidentifiable.

Furthermore, government disclosure of its own video footage isn't helping to maintain belief: It's actually better for UFOs when ufologists can claim that "the powers that be know everything and are hiding it from us" rather than seeing that the government appears to have basically the same info about UFOs as the public: namely grainy, inconclusive visual evidence.

11. Where is everybody

Like Newton and the apple or George Washington and the cherry tree, one day in 1950, the physicist and Nobel Laureate, Enrico Fermi sat down to lunch with colleagues at the Fuller Lodge at Los Alamos National Laboratory in New Mexico and came up with a powerful argument about the existence of extraterrestrial intelligence, the so-called "Fermi paradox." This story has since become a kind of a legend, although like Newton's apple, the story is only partly true.

The physicist Eric Jones published the recollections of the physicist's luncheon companions more than thirty-five years later. Accordingly, during the walk to the Fuller Lodge, the physicists discussed a recent spate of UFO sightings, and a cartoon in the New Yorker Magazine depicting aliens and a flying saucer. Although the topic of conversation moved on as the group sat down for lunch, Edward Teller recalls "in the middle of the conversation, Fermi came out with the quite unexpected question...

Where is everybody?

The result of his question was general laughter because of the strange fact that in spite of Fermi's question coming out of the clear blue, everybody around the table seemed to understand at once that he was talking about extraterrestrial life."

Fermi, who had won a Nobel Prize in 1938, was famous for his ability to estimate pretty good answers to tough questions using very little data and back-of-the-envelope calculations.

In one well-known example, he estimated the strength of the blast created by the first nuclear test explosion by dropping small pieces of paper during it and watching how far they travelled through the air. This allowed him to calculate the change in air pressure caused by the blast, which in turn meant he could work out the amount of energy released. His rough estimate that the explosion was the equivalent of 10,000 tons of TNT was not too far off the real figure of 21,000 tons.

The Fermi paradox is commonly understood as asking why extraterrestrials have not visited Earth, but the same reasoning applies to the question of why signals from extraterrestrials have not been heard. SETI, the Search for Extraterrestrial Intelligence is a collective term for scientific searches for intelligent extraterrestrial and is just another version of the same question, sometimes referred to as "the Great Silence."

Fermi didn't actually calculate the probability of extraterrestrial life but in 1961 the Cornell University astronomer, Frank Drake, presented an equation that identified specific factors thought to play a role in the development of such civilizations. The technique Fermi turned to for the question of extraterrestrial life is as follows: -

1. The Milky Way contains hundreds of billions of stars, and billions of them are similar to the sun.

2. It is highly likely that some of these stars will have planets that are similar to Earth.

3. If we assume – via the Copernican principle – that Earth is not particularly special, then intelligent life should also exist on some fraction of these Earth-like planets.

4. Some of these intelligent life-forms might develop advanced technology, and even interstellar travel.

5. Interstellar travel would take a long time, but as there are many sun-like stars that are billions of years older, there has been plenty of time for such travel to have occurred.

6. Given all this, why haven't we met or seen any trace of aliens? Where is everybody?

The Fermi paradox can be stated more completely like this:

The size and age of the universe incline us to believe that many technologically advanced civilizations must exist. However, this belief seems logically inconsistent with our lack of observational evidence to support it. Either,

> *(1) the initial assumption is incorrect and technologically advanced intelligent life is much rarer than we believe, or*

(2) our current observations are incomplete, and we simply have not detected them yet, or

(3) our search methodologies are flawed, and we are not searching for the correct indicators.

As already said, SETI is the scientific searches for intelligent extraterrestrial life, for example, monitoring electromagnetic radiation for signs of transmissions from civilizations on other planets. Scientific investigation began shortly after the advent of radio in the early 1900s, and focused international efforts have been going on since the 1980.

There have been many earlier searches for extraterrestrial intelligence within the Solar System. In 1896, Nikola Tesla suggested that an extreme version of his wireless electrical transmission system could be used to contact beings on Mars. In 1899, while conducting experiments at his Colorado Springs experimental station, he thought he had detected a signal from that planet since an odd repetitive static signal seemed to cut off when Mars set in the night sky.

Analysis of Tesla's research has ranged from suggestions that Tesla detected nothing, he simply misunderstood the new technology he was working with, to claims that Tesla may have been observing signals from Marconi's European radio experiments and even that he could have picked up naturally occurring Jovian plasma torus signals.

In 1960, Frank Drake performed the first modern SETI experiment, named "Project Ozma", Drake used a radio telescope 85 foot in diameter at Green Bank, West Virginia, to examine the stars Tau Ceti and Epsilon Eridani near the 1.420 gigahertz marker frequency, a region of the radio spectrum dubbed the "water hole." He found nothing of interest.

The Ohio State SETI program gained fame on August 15, 1977, when Jerry Ehman, a project volunteer, witnessed a startlingly strong signal received by the telescope. He quickly circled the indication on a printout and scribbled the exclamation "Wow!" in the margin. Dubbed the Wow! signal, it is considered by some to be the best candidate for a radio signal from an artificial, extraterrestrial source ever discovered, but it has not been detected again in several additional searches.

Many radio frequencies penetrate Earth's atmosphere quite well, and this led to radio telescopes that investigate the cosmos using large radio antennas. Furthermore, human endeavours emit considerable electromagnetic radiation as a by-product of communications such as television and radio. These signals would be easy to recognize as artificial due to their repetitive nature and narrow bandwidths. If this is typical, one way of discovering an extraterrestrial civilization might be to detect artificial radio emissions from a location outside the Solar System.

The search for extraterrestrial intelligence, is a numbers game, and the bigger the numbers the better they are. The more places we look for alien beings — the more expansive we search — the greater the chance we'll turn up proof of their existence. So, it's notable that Breakthrough Listen, a privately funded, decade-long research project based at the University of California, Berkeley, just announced a significant number of new observations. And while the researchers didn't uncover any signals from extraterrestrials, they've taken a major step forward in the search.

SETI's basic premise, we live in a galaxy festooned with brainy societies rests upon the hypothesis that there must be many habitats in the Milky Way where complex biology has had a chance to evolve and thrive. Drake, himself stated that given the uncertainties, there are probably between 1000 and 100,000,000 civilizations in the Milky Way galaxy alone. Even if this estimate is hundreds or thousands of times too optimistic, there could still be plenty of aliens to find.

But if this straw-man argument suggests that extraterrestrials are out there, it also suggests that detecting them will require a lot of searching. The new results from Breakthrough Listen — an examination of roughly 1,300 nearby stars — has approximately doubled the tally of reconnoitered real estate. This was not a trivial effort; it took scientists three years of heavy-duty work using large antennas in West Virginia and Australia. For each of these star systems, they carefully sifted through several billion radio channels, looking for a signal of the type that only a radio transmitter can produce.

No extraterrestrial radio emissions have ever been detected ...

to date.

But what if extraterrestrials really did arrive, what if we should really discover an alien civilization – are we ready, what are the consequences for our race if we encountered extraterrestrial life?

Remember the H.G. Wells' War of the Worlds – "scenes" depicting chaos, panic, and hysteria. Buildings crumble, fires rage, riots break out, societies collapse. In fiction, it's worth noting the discovery of extraterrestrial life is portrayed as having negative societal or psychological consequences.

I suspect; however, the answer lies in whether aliens take the form of harmless microbes found on planets like Mars versus being confronted with an advanced, technological alien race. Most don't regard microscopic extraterrestrials as either threatening or enlightening.

The potential impact from extraterrestrial contact could vary greatly in magnitude and type, based on the extraterrestrial civilization's level of technological advancement, degree of benevolence or malevolence, and level of mutual comprehension between itself and humanity. The medium through which we are contacted, be it electromagnetic radiation, direct physical interaction, extraterrestrial artefact, or otherwise, may also influence the impact of contact. Incorporating these factors, various systems have been created to assess the implications of extraterrestrial contact.

The implications of extraterrestrial contact, particularly with a technologically superior civilization, have often been likened to the meeting of two vastly different human cultures on Earth, such as for example was the widespread transfer of plants, animals, culture, human populations, technology, diseases, and ideas between the Americas, West Africa, and the Old World in the 15th and 16th centuries.

Such meetings have generally led to the destruction of the civilization receiving contact (as opposed to the "contactor", which initiates contact), and therefore destruction of human civilization is a possible outcome. Extraterrestrial contact is also analogous to the numerous encounters between non-human native and invasive species occupying the same ecological niche. However, the absence of verified public contact to date means tragic consequences are still largely speculative.

I doubt, very much, that contact with other intelligent life will cause terrestrial religion to collapse. However, that's not to say challenges to traditional doctrinal belief are not likely to be raised. Like for example:

a. What's the scope of God's creation?

b. What can we expect regarding the moral character of extraterrestrial beings?

c. Is one earthly incarnation in Jesus Christ enough for the entire cosmos, or should we expect multiple incarnations on multiple planets?

More than probable contact with extra-terrestrial intelligence will expand the Bible's vision so that all of creation, including the 13.7 billion-year history of the universe replete with all of God's creatures.

On the question of whether we are ready. What might be the first few steps we may take on confirmation of extraterrestrial life. Work has already begun to develop a set of protocols that address how news of contact could be communicated; Sensitively, and in a measured, considered, and importantly, quantifiable way.

The Rio Scale is a tool used by astronomers searching for extraterrestrial intelligence to help communicate to the public 'how excited' they should be about what has been observed. The Scale measures the consequences for humans if the signal is from aliens, as well as the probability that the signal really is from aliens, and not a natural phenomenon or human-made. The scale gives a score between zero and ten, so that the public can quickly see how important a signal really is. I'm not sure if this has been developed with a sense of optimisms, the sharing of joy and good will or indeed taken to communicate danger and impending doom.

The protocol is a scale that can accompany reports of any claims of the detection of extraterrestrial intelligence. The scale, called Rio Version 2, aims to bring consensus across academic disciplines, when classifying signals potentially indicating the existence of advanced extraterrestrial life. This scale should convey both the significance and credibility of the claimed detection in the same manner as the Richter scale is a measure of the size of an

force majeure.

———————

www.ingramcontent.com/pod-product-compliance
Lightning Source LLC
Chambersburg PA
CBHW072050280526
45788CB00006B/2243